Getting a Job in
New Zealand

# Getting a Job in
# New Zealand

*Find well-paid work
and a great new lifestyle*

**JOY MUIRHEAD**
*2nd edition*

**How To Books**

Published by How To Books Ltd, 3 Newtec Place,
Magdalen Road, Oxford OX4 1RE. United Kingdom.
Tel: (01865) 793806. Fax: (01865) 248780.
email: info@howtobooks.co.uk
http://www.howtobooks.co.uk

First endition 1996
Second edition 2000

British Library Cataloguing in Publication Data
A catalogue record for this book is available from the British
Library

Edited by Christine Kinsman
Cover design by Shireen Nathoo Design
Cover image PhotoDisc
Cover copy by Sallyann Sheridan

Produced for How To Books by Deer Park Productions
Typeset by PDQ Typesetting, Stoke-on-Trent, Staffs.
Printed and bound by The Cromwell Press, Trowbridge,
Wiltshire

NOTE: The material contained in this book is set out in good
faith for general guidance and no liability can be accepted
for loss or expense incurred as a result of relying in particular
circumstances on statements made in the book. Laws and
regulations are complex and liable to change, and readers should
check the current position with the relevant authorities before
making personal arrangements.

# Contents

Preface                                                          10

**1 Choosing New Zealand**                                       **13**
Understanding the Treaty of Waitangi                             13
Recognising Maori phrases                                        14
Introducing New Zealand                                          15
Population trends                                                15
Climatic trends                                                  16
The cities                                                       17
Agriculture                                                      17
Case studies                                                     18
Points for discussion                                            19

**2 Understanding the economy**                                  **20**
Understanding the New Zealand economy                            20
Introducing the current situation                                20
Coping with unemployment                                         21
Case studies                                                     23
Points for discussion                                            24

**3 Immigration**                                                **25**
Knowing the trends                                               25
Visas and permits                                                26
Understanding the temporary visitors category                    27
Understanding the temporary visitors (student) category          28
Understanding the long term business category                    29
Understanding the temporary visitors (temporary workers)
category                                                         30
Applying for work permits                                        30
Applying for a visitor's visa                                    31
United Kingdom citizens' working holiday scheme                  32

Permanent migrants                                                  33
Becoming a permanent migrant                                        34
Becoming a permanent migrant – General Skills Category              35
Becoming a permanent migrant – Business Investor Category           41
Becoming a permanent migrant – Entrepreneur Category                48
Becoming a permanent migrant – Family Category                      49
Becoming a permanent migrant – Humanitarian Category                50
Case studies                                                        51
Points for discussion                                               52

**4 Understanding employment conditions and law                     53**
Signing a contract                                                  53
Joining a union                                                     54
Handling a personal grievance                                       55
Knowing your rights                                                 56
Taking maternity leave                                              56
Case studies                                                        56
Points for discussion                                               57

**5 Your workplace environment                                      58**
Finding your niche                                                  58
Smokefree                                                           58
Working with computers                                              59
Coping with accidents                                               59
Keeping safe and healthy                                            59
Case studies                                                        60
Points for discussion                                               61

**6 Paying tax                                                       62**
Paying personal tax                                                 62
Pay as you earn                                                     62
Paying provisional tax                                              63
Paying goods and services tax                                       64
Paying company tax                                                  65
Paying tax on fringe benefits                                       66
Avoiding double taxation                                            66
Bringing capital with you                                           67
Setting up your pension                                             67
Getting family support                                              67
Case studies                                                        67
Points for discussion                                               68

7 **Settling in** **69**
  Finding accommodation 69
  Knowing the schooling system 69
  Becoming a kiwi 71
  Playing the game 72
  Case studies 73
  Points for discussion 74

8 **Careers and professions** **75**
  Is this you? 75
  Getting started 76
  Finding job leads 79
  Tackling typical interview questions 79
  Choosing your occupation 80
  Personnel consultants 101
  Meeting New Zealand qualification requirements 105
  Case studies 105
  Points for discussion 106

9 **Retraining** **107**
  Finding training assistance 107
  Going to university 107
  Training at a polytechnic college 109
  Central Institute of Technology (CIT) 109
  Advanced Vocational Awards and Trade Certification Board
  examinations 110
  Case studies 111
  Points for discussion 111

10 **Understanding the New Zealand health structure** **112**
  Ministry of Health 112
  Regional health authorities 112
  Crown Health Enterprises (hospitals) 113
  Getting dental care 113
  Applying for accident compensation 113
  Health care for long-term visitors 114
  Health care for short-term visitors 115
  Covering yourself with medical insurance 115
  Case studies 116
  Points for discussion 117

**11 Summing up**                                  **118**
    Advantages                                118
    Disadvantages                             118
    Checklist for action                      119

Appendix                                      **120**
    Employment agencies                       120
    Employment contract negotiators           127
    Immigration consultants                   128
    Professional associations                 131
    Trade and/or industry associations        132

Glossary                                      135

Useful addresses                              137

Further reading                               140

Index                                         142

# List of Illustrations

1    Redundancy                                               22

2    Number of people approved for residence 1992/3–1998/99   25

3    Personal grievance claims                                55

4    A selection of property advertisements                   70

5    Sample functional CV                                     77

6    Sample chronological CV                                  78

# Preface

Now, *here*, you see, it takes all the running *you* can do, to keep in the same place. If you want to get somewhere else, you must run at least twice as fast as that! (The Red Queen to Alice in Lewis Carroll's *Through the Looking-Glass*.)

In New Zealand we are twelve hours ahead of the United Kingdom. Because of this it would seem that we do indeed spend our time running fast. So far we have managed to run half a day away from England, and we are still running!

New Zealanders pride themselves on being 'all-rounders' and the New Zealand armed forces service overseas have always been acclaimed as being extremely adaptable. New Zealand nannies are well sought after around the world because they can change nappies, clean a four-bedroom house, look after the toddlers and cook a four-course meal while drinking their morning coffee!

There is a much abused buzz term in force in New Zealand – 'flexibility'. It applies to everyone except the hierarchy. Whenever you find yourself faced with a situation in which you are required to be 'flexible', always be sure to have the exact parameters of 'flexible' detailed in writing.

I have found the workplace environment throughout my employment experiences here to be challenging, enabling me to extend my skills tenfold. Extra training is readily available, and there is no excuse for saying 'Sorry, I haven't been shown how to do that.' If you are willing to progress then you will find the opportunities to improve your skills.

I hope you find a niche for yourself within the New Zealand workforce. Always remember – it's not 'What can New Zealand do for me?' but 'What can *I* do for New Zealand?'

Whilst preparing the second edition of this book I have tried to include email and website addresses wherever possible.

At the end of November 1999 there was a general election, and as a result, a change of government. There will obviously be many policy changes because of this, and I urge you to check with New Zealand Immigration for the latest details to ensure new policies do not alter your application procedures. Changes happen a lot faster in New Zealand than they do in England.

Finally I would like to express my thanks to the following organisations for giving so much valuable help and advice during the preparation of this book:

New Zealand Immigration Service
Lampen Group Ltd
IDPE Consultants
Rob Law Consultants
Department of Statistics
New Zealand Employment Service

*Joy Muirhead*

# 1

## Choosing New Zealand

### UNDERSTANDING THE TREATY OF WAITANGI

As a new migrant in New Zealand you will automatically be affected by the Treaty of Waitangi. Your right to settle here comes from the British right to settle and govern which was obtained through the Treaty.

The Treaty of Waitangi now affects many areas of life in New Zealand. When applying for a job, particularly in a government department, you may be asked what you know of the Treaty and its implications. At school your children may be taught the Maori language, Treaty issues and bi-cultural values.

You should know the Treaty exists and what it means. You should also know that in New Zealand there are different interpretations and views of the Treaty. Living in New Zealand you have a responsibility through the Treaty of Waitangi to protect the social, political, cultural and spiritual rights of the Maori people.

Waitangi Day, 6 February, is a public holiday in New Zealand.

### What is the Treaty?

On 6 February 1840, at Waitangi in the Bay of Islands, a treaty was signed between two sovereign states: the United Kingdom of Great Britain and Ireland (the British Crown), and the United Tribes of New Zealand and other tribal leaders (Maori).

The British Crown gained the right of governorship and the right to settle in New Zealand. Maori kept authority over their lands and all their affairs and gained the rights of British citizens.

To understand the history of New Zealand and the current patterns of social relationships between people, you need to know about the Treaty and the attitudes of the two main parties at the time of the signing and today.

Known habitation of New Zealand dates back over one thousand years. Maori are the indigenous people or tangata whenua of New Zealand. The first European exploration was in 1769 and led whalers and traders, missionaries and finally European settlers to New Zealand. The Treaty of Waitangi established a partnership between the Maori people of New Zealand and the new settlers, providing a framework for Maori and non-Maori to live in this country together. The Treaty reaffirmed Maori rights and set up a national government which would help in the settlement of New Zealand.

## Different emphases

The Treaty is in two texts, one English and one Maori, and one is not an exact translation of the other. The Treaty is made up of a preamble followed by three articles and an epilogue. Most Maori signed the Maori version and it is this version that has authority, or mana, amongst most Maori. The English version was taken back to Britain and made legal in the British sense.

In the preamble the objectives are stated:

• to protect Maori interests

• to provide British settlement

• to set up a government to maintain peace and order.

The Maori version gives a different emphasis. It suggests the British Crown's main promise to Maori was to preserve the chiefs and tribes in their proper rank and status. The Treaty gives responsibilities and obligations to each Treaty partner. To this end it is important that non-Maori realise the Treaty belongs to them just as much as it does to Maori.

## RECOGNISING MAORI PHRASES

The Government declared 1995 the Maori language year. It has been very evident in the growing use of everyday Maori greetings and phrases:

| | |
|---|---|
| *Kia ora* | Hello |
| *Tena koutou* | Hello (to a group of people) |
| *Ka kite ano* | See you again |
| *Haere Mai* | Welcome |
| *Haere ra* | Goodbye (to the person leaving) |

## INTRODUCING NEW ZEALAND

New Zealand lies in the Southern Pacific Ocean, 1,600 km east of Australia. It is made up of the North and South Islands and a number of smaller islands, with a total land area of 266,171 sq km. Mountain ranges and hill country dominate New Zealand's landscape; one of the most striking physical features is the Southern Alps. These, along with fiords, glaciers and lakes, and the coastal plains of Canterbury and Southlands, add to the variety of the South Island scenery.

In the North Island, the volcanic interior contains New Zealand's largest lake, Lake Taupo, and most of the country's active volcanoes – Ruapehu, which erupted in September 1995, caused high-speed mud flows (lahars) which contaminated rivers and streams. Red-hot rocks the size of cars were spewed forth and the very successful skiing season was brought to an abrupt halt. Ash closed the main trunk road north and airports around the region were forced to close because of ash. Ngauruhoe and Tongariro which lie close by are dormant but White Island which lies off the coast of the Bay of Plenty is also active. Hot springs, geysers and mudpools also form part of the volcanic system centred around Rotorua.

## POPULATION TRENDS

### The 'drift to the north'

Following the end of the gold boom in the South Island in the 1890s, the proportion of the total population living in the South Island began steadily to decrease. From the 1896 Census onward the population of the North Island has exceeded that of the South.

Since that time the North Island's population has continued to expand at a greater rate, and its share of the total population has continued to grow (see p. 17).

Auckland is a key region in internal migration patterns, gaining population at the expense of most other regions. The second major region for receiving migrants is Waikato.

In most cases population flows favoured regions to the north. Thus, Southland lost population to Otago, Otago to Canterbury, Canterbury lost to Wellington and Wellington lost to Auckland.

### Other migration flows

The significance of the 'drift to the north', however, must be put in perspective. Internal migration is not a one-way process. Typically, for each migration stream, moving in one direction there is an opposing counter stream. Further, a sizeable proportion of internal migration occurs between adjacent regions. The major flows over long distances, however, are mainly between major urban areas. The balance of urban and rural components is another major feature of New Zealand's changing demography.

### What causes population changes?
Many influences have contributed to the persistence and amplification of the population differential between the two islands. The North Island has had a higher birth rate, a lower mortality rate and, as a result, a higher rate of natural increase. In addition, the bulk of overseas migrants settle in the North Island.

## CLIMATIC TRENDS
Seasons are opposite to the northern hemisphere, with January and February the warmest months and July the coldest. The climate is temperate – averages range from 7 degrees C in July to 16 degrees C in January – but summer temperatures reach the low 30s in many places. The mean average rainfall varies widely – from less than 400 mm in the Central Otago (South Island) to over 12,000 mm in the Southern Alps. For most of the North Island and the northern South Island the driest season is summer. However, for the west coast and much of inland Canterbury (South Island), Otago and Southland, winter is the driest season.

|  | Mean daily maximum temperature | | Bright sunshine hours | Mean annual rainfall mm |
|---|---|---|---|---|
|  | Jan. °C | July | | |
| Auckland | 23.8 | 14.7 | 2,118 | 1,253 |
| Wellington | 20.4 | 11.2 | 2,044 | 1,264 |
| Christchurch | 22.5 | 11.1 | 2,057 | 644 |
| Dunedin | 19.0 | 9.9 | 1,596 | 788 |

1994 was an extreme year for climate. In eastern Northland (North Island) and Hawkes Bay (North Island), it was the driest year since records began in the nineteenth century. For most places, 1993 was a very sunny year. 1994 was not as cold as either 1992 or 1993.

The far north of the North Island is regarded as semi-tropical, with temperatures averaging 16 degrees. The extremes can be a low of 14 and a high of 30. Auckland has an average temperature of 15 degrees, with extremes of a low of 12 degrees and a high of 28 degrees. In these two areas you will experience a fairly high humidity level. Put simply, the temperature in the lower half of the South Island is equivalent to the temperatures in the north of Scotland, and the temperatures in the North of the North Island are similar to, although slightly hotter and more humid than, the south of England.

## THE CITIES

Dunedin and Christchurch are both university cities, and there is an interesting hub of activity which is generated by university life. Dunedin was settled by the early Scottish settlers and still retains the Scottish flavour. Christchurch however is very English, more English some say than England.

| New Zealand population | |
|---|---:|
| Total | 3,792,000 |
| North Island | 2,866,300 |
| South Island | 925,700 |
| *Main centres* | |
| Auckland (NI) | 1,076,100 |
| Wellington (NI) | 346,400 |
| Christchurch (SI) | 339,500 |
| Hamilton (NI) | 167,200 |
| Dunedin (SI) | 112,400 |

## AGRICULTURE

In the South Island sheep farming is the main form of pastoral agriculture with a sprinkling of beef cattle in the high and hill country and wetter flat areas, and some dairying on the flat land of both coasts.

Fruit farming is extensive in both islands. In the South Island the main regions planted in fruit are:

| Otago | Apricots, nectarines |
| Marlborough and Otago | Cherries |
| Canterbury | Blackcurrants, raspberries |
| Tasman | Boysenberries  . |
| Marlborough | Outdoor grapes |
| Nelson | European pears, apples |

In the North Island the fruit growing areas are:

| Bay of Plenty | Grapefruit, lemons, tangelos, kiwifruit, passionfruit |
| Northland | Mandarins |
| Gisborne and Northland | Oranges |
| Hawkes Bay | Apples, pears, nectarines, peaches |
| Bay of Plenty and Auckland | Nashi, avocados, feijoas |
| Auckland and Hawkes Bay | Plums |
| Waikato | Blueberries |
| Auckland | Strawberries, persimmons |
| Bay of Plenty and Northland | Tamarillos |
| Hawkes Bay and Gisborne | Outdoor grapes |

## CASE STUDIES

### Kerry complains

Kerry Watson was a young woman who was training to be a nurse. She objected to the Maori teaching in the cultural safety section of her nurse training. She was outspoken, and said that she felt the trainees were being bombarded with the Maori cultural sensitivity, while the obvious requirements, e.g. knowing how to bandage a broken limb and other medical procedures, were being bypassed by the training organisation. She was harshly treated and it was said that she didn't pass the cultural safety portion of the course, and therefore wasn't fit to be a nurse. She eventually went to Australia where she is now working in her chosen profession as a very well respected nurse.

### The Wright family make the wrong choice

John Wright and his wife and two children decided that Invercargill would be the best place to live and work. They were offered two job situations, one in Invercargill in the South Island and one in Kawerau in the North Island. The organisation that offered the two teaching positions told John that Invercargill was the best place to be as Kawerau was full of foreigners. John and his family settled in Invercargill and waited for the rain to stop. It rained for almost six weeks non-stop. In the meantime his friends in Kawerau basked in warm sub-tropical weather, even though it was early winter. The Wright family regretted their decision and the fact that they hadn't properly researched the place they had chosen.

*Note:*
The immigration department nearest to you can help with this information. It's easier and cheaper to change your mind on paper that it is to pack your belongings and move.

## Peter Jones returns
Peter had left New Zealand with big ambitions in his chosen career of acting. He had felt a certain amount of restraint in New Zealand. He enjoyed working in England and found many interesting acting opportunities and filled in with part-time jobs in between. After six years away he decided that it was time to bring his English wife back to New Zealand with him to raise his young family. Peter soon realised after a month of searching for acting opportunities that they were few and far between. His wife and two young children were not finding it easy to fit into the new lifestyle so after three months they returned to England. Peter is now happily settled once more in England.

## POINTS FOR DISCUSSION

1. As a non New Zealander, would you readily accept the importance of things 'Maori', and be prepared to try to understand and work within the meaning of the Treaty of Waitangi?

2. Could you accept the situation that your child may be required to learn the Maori language at school?

3. The government has sanctioned a new terminology, 'cultural safety', and it creeps into many everyday situations. Nurses, for example, have to undergo a course in 'cultural safety' and be examined on its content and their application of it, before they can be registered. Cultural safety is about knowing what the Maori will and will not expect and accept when they are faced with sickness. It is in fact a course that makes you aware of their sensitivity, and not as one would expect, the sensitivity of all other races in equal proportion. Could you work with this situation?

# 2

## Understanding the Economy

### UNDERSTANDING THE NEW ZEALAND ECONOMY

Describing and analysing the New Zealand economy requires considerable subtlety. In comparison with some of the economies with which we interact most, New Zealand's is small and simple, yet the value of activity in New Zealand is large and complex. The goods and services produced and consumed in New Zealand have many characteristics in common with those of other economies (indeed they are often identical) and yet the New Zealand economy must be understood in its own context and nature rather than merely fitted into international classifications.

New Zealand's cultural, political and social institutions are much indebted to the Maori heritage, to what was brought by the predominantly British immigrants and to what has been developed within New Zealand by local activity shaped by a continuing inflow of ideas and people. The economy, however, owes very little to the Maori heritage. Rather, Maori have had to adapt to participate in the economy, and current efforts to rectify departures from the provisions of the Treaty of Waitangi owe a great deal to the injustices that accompanied that process, most of them being unintended.

### INTRODUCING THE CURRENT SITUATION

In 1998 the government removed tariffs on fully assembled cars coming into the country. This resulted in a huge downturn in business for the car assembly plants, and many closed.

The tariff cuts have also hit the textile manufacturing companies, and New Zealand's largest, Bendon, have closed and moved to Asia, saying they can no longer afford to manufacture in New Zealand.

Over the last year the New Zealand economy has been affected by several factors: Asian, high interest rates and the depreciation of the NZ$ against most overseas currencies. There has also been some depreciation against the US$. Against the Aust$ we are fairly stable.

The economy is forecast to grow an average of 3% in each of the next three years. That is expected to equal 115,000 new jobs, many of which are expected to be in service areas, supporting growing industries like tourism and telecommunications.
The New Zealand economy was recently likened to running the rapids. There has been a trip through torrid and turbulent waters. Some did not make it, but the stronger ones, with resolute determination did. We survived the rapids and are now turning the bend to calmer waters, which will in turn, hopefully mean more stable growth.

## COPING WITH UNEMPLOYMENT

At the year ended March 1998, the following table shows the employment situation according to New Zealand Statistics figures.

| Labour force | | | | |
|---|---|---|---|---|
| | | **Average for March quarter** | | |
| | | **1996** | **1997** | **1998** |
| **Total labour force** | **(0000)** | **1,892.5** | **1,858.0** | **1,872.4** |
| Males | (0000) | 1,014.5 | 1,025.6 | 1,034.8 |
| Females | (000) | 815.0 | 832.5 | 837.6 |
| Unemployment rate | % | 6.5 | 6.8 | 7.5 |
| Males | % | 6.4 | 6.5 | 7.4 |
| Females | % | 6.6 | 7.3 | 7.7 |
| | | **At mid February** | | |
| **Average ordinary time weekly earnings** | | **1996** | **1997** | **1998** |
| Males | $/wk | 667.84 | 692.80 | 706.20 |
| Females | $/wk | 512.87 | 533.20 | 548.42 |
| **Employed labour force** | **$/wk** | **597.43** | **619.98** | **633.57** |

Interesting facts:

| | |
|---|---|
| NZ population mid 1998 | 3.8m |
| UK population mid 1998 | 58.2m |
| NZ unemployment rate mid 1998 | 7.3% |
| UK unemployment rate mid 1998 | 6.4% |
| NZ physicians per 1,000 population | 2.1 |
| UK physicians per 1,000 population | 1.6 |

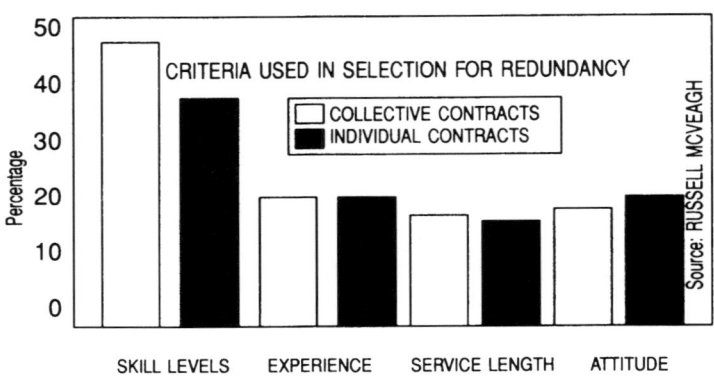

## REDUNDANCY SELECTION

CRITERIA USED IN SELECTION FOR REDUNDANCY

☐ COLLECTIVE CONTRACTS
■ INDIVIDUAL CONTRACTS

Percentage

50
40
30
20
10
0

SKILL LEVELS     EXPERIENCE     SERVICE LENGTH     ATTITUDE

Source: RUSSELL MCVEAGH

Most firms select people for redundancy on the basis of skill levels, the survey by law firm Russell McVeagh shows. This was true of 46 per cent of redundancies made under collective employment contracts and 36 per cent under individual contracts. The employee's attitude was a factor in 17 per cent of redundancies made under individual contracts, but only 11 per cent under collective contracts. Experience was the next most common criterion followed by length of service.

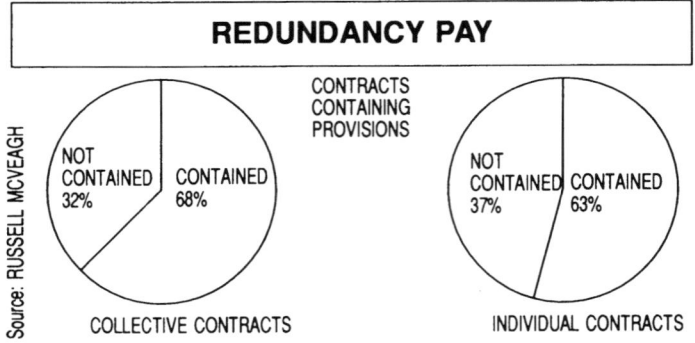

## REDUNDANCY PAY

Source: RUSSELL MCVEAGH

CONTRACTS CONTAINING PROVISIONS

NOT CONTAINED 32%     CONTAINED 68%

COLLECTIVE CONTRACTS

NOT CONTAINED 37%     CONTAINED 63%

INDIVIDUAL CONTRACTS

Most collective and individual employment contracts contain provisions outlining how much employees will be paid if they are made redundant, the survey shows. The most common formula for redundancy compensation in collective contracts was six weeks' pay for the first year of service and two weeks for each subsequent year. The most common formula in individual contracts was four weeks' pay for the first year of service and two weeks' for each subsequent year.

Fig. 1. Redundancy.

## Increase in average total hourly earnings

Average total hourly earnings increased by 23 cents or 1.3 per cent between May 1999 and August 1999, latest figures from *Statistics New Zealand* show. Average total hourly earnings now total $17.95. The quarterly increase was driven mainly by composition changes rather than increases in wages. In the period May 1999 to August 1999 there was a significant change in the distribution of hours paid across industries. Although total hours paid decreased overall, relatively more hours were paid in industries that have higher average earnings.

Several industries contributed to the increase including: property and business services; wholesale trade and retail trade; personal and other services; transport, storage and communication; and education. There was a partially offsetting decrease in the manufacturing industry.

Private sector average ordinary time hourly earnings also increased by 1.3. per cent between May 1999 and August 1999 and are now $16.90. In the year to August 1999, private sector average ordinary time hourly earnings have increased 3.1 per cent.

## CASE STUDIES

### Ngaire has a problem

Ngaire had always wanted her own home. She saved for many years until she had enough deposit to start looking for a home. She finally found a well-built two-bedroomed bungalow that was under $100,000. She was able to get a mortgage based upon the fact that she was fully employed.

After she had been in her house for five years her mortgage interest rate was raised. Ngaire had to seriously consider selling her home, but after careful budgeting she was able to keep paying her mortgage. Fortunately a few months later the mortgage rate dropped to the level it had been when she first began her payments. The firm Ngaire worked for began laying off people three years later, and she found that she was to have her hours cut by half. However, by this time she was freehold, and only had to pay for her expenses, rates and food. She managed to find other part-time work to fit in with her main job.

### Stuart goes back to study

Stuart and Amy had been married for six years when Stuart's firm began laying off some workers. Stuart and Amy decided that they would have to take a long hard look at their situation. Amy had been working in a kindergarten part time, but when her baby was born she had to stay at home for a year to look after him. Stuart decided that the future didn't look rosy for commercial property valuers, and decided to take a computer course. After his course of study was completed he was able to find a job as a computer programmer. He knew he had entered a very competitive field, but he was happy to keep updating his skills as necessary.

### Jean tries to upgrade her skills

Jean had always been self-employed. When her marriage broke up she and her husband had to sell their catering business in order to share the proceeds. Jean had to find a job, but she had no qualifications.

When she was 17 she had worked in an office, but that was several years before she had married and had a family. She was forced to put her name down for unemployment benefit, and listed the limited skills she had. The only type of work she could find was helping out in cafés, washing mountains of dishes and cleaning floors. This work finally ceased and she tried to find more work but to no avail. After six months unemployment the Labour Department contacted her and told her that because she had been unemployed for six months she was eligible for free skills training. They asked her what she would like to do, and she said she would like to update her office skills.

They put her on a 12-month word-processing course, and when she had finished she was able to get a good secretarial job, and now she is confidently looking forward to a good future.

### POINTS FOR DISCUSSION

1. Mortgage rates do not always remain firm. Could you budget for fluctuations?

2. If you were made redundant, would you consider retraining in another field?

3. Would you be prepared to study in your free time in another skill field?

# 3

## Immigration

**KNOWING THE TRENDS**

### Residence approvals

The graph below shows the number of people approved for residence each financial year since 1992/93. The government's immigration target for the 1998/99 financial year was 38,000 (plus or minus 10 per cent) with the objective of achieving an average net gain of 10,000 people a year over the medium term (5–10 years).

The number of people approved for residence in the 1998/99 financial year was 30,583 (provisional). In the preceding years the totals were: 1997/98 – 31,542; 1996/97 – 33,836; 1995/96 – 54,654; 1994/95 – 50,752; 1993/94 – 33,514; and 1992/93 – 29,649.

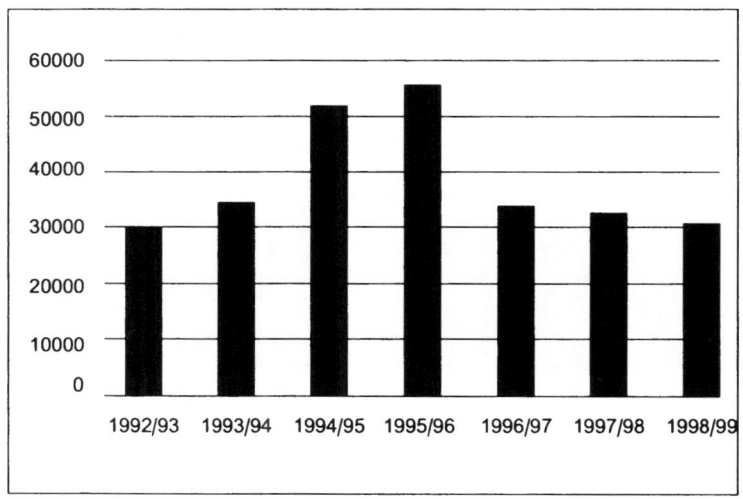

Fig. 2. Number of people approved for residence 1992/93–1998/99.
Source: *Statistics NZ*.

### Region of origin
A total of 30,583 people were approved for residence in New Zealand in the financial year ended 30 June 1999. This compares with a total of 31,542 people approved for residence in the previous year. People from Europe made up the largest regional group of migrants in 1998/99 with 22% of the total, followed by people from the Middle East and Africa with 18%, and North Asia and the Pacific each contributing 16%. The largest regional group for the 1997/98 year was also from Europe (24%) but north Asia was in second position (20%).

### Country of origin
During the past two financial years the top of the list for people approved for residence was Great Britain with 4,357 people, or 14% of the total. South Africa was next with 3,595 (12%), followed by China with 3,354 (11%).

## VISAS AND PERMITS

Visas and permits can be applied for in the following categories:

- visitor's visa/visitor's permit
- student visa/student permit
- residence visa/residence permit
- returning residence visa
- long term business visa/permit.

### Visas
A visa is an endorsement placed in your passport or certificate of identity before your departure for New Zealand. Visas allow travel to New Zealand until the date specified. They do not give permission to be in New Zealand, but rather indicate that the holder has permission to travel to the country, and that the issuing officer knows of no reason why a permit should not be issued on arrival. It is possible, however, that even a person with a visa will not automatically be granted entry to New Zealand. In the vast majority of cases, visas are issued overseas. The major exception to this is visas issued in New Zealand for re-entry purposes.

## Permits

A permit gives the holder permission to be in the country for a specific purpose. It lapses when the holder leaves the country, obtains another permit, or the permit is revoked for some reason. **Permits can only be granted within New Zealand.**

## Grounds for refusal

The Immigration Act defines classes of people who are not eligible for a permit or a visa. These include those who:

- have ever been convicted and sentenced to prison for five years or more

- have been convicted and sentenced to prison for twelve months or more in the past ten years

- have been deported from any country or convicted of any immigration offence

- have been removed from New Zealand and whose removal warrant or order is still in force

- are suspected by the authorities of being a terrorist, or a person who is likely to commit a crime or be a danger to New Zealand.

You are likely to be refused a residence visa or permit, if you have been convicted of any offences. These grounds for refusal relating to conviction continue to apply, even if the conviction has been taken off the record.

If you are in New Zealand unlawfully, you are not eligible to apply for residence unless the transitional provisions of the Immigration Amendment Act 1991 apply to you.

## UNDERSTANDING THE TEMPORARY VISITORS CATEGORY

Temporary visitors are people who are in New Zealand for a specified amount of time, and who must leave at the end of that time, unless they have obtained a further permit.

Temporary visitors include:

1. *Visitors* – people coming to the country as tourists for example, or to visit friends or family.

2. *Students* – those who come to New Zealand specifically to

undertake a course of study of three months or more.

3. *Temporary workers* – people with a work permit, enabling them to be employed in a specified type of work for either all or part of their stay.

Visitors who do not apply in advance for a longer stay are usually only permitted to be in New Zealand for a stay of up to six months in any twelve-month period. All visitors are required to stay outside New Zealand for a period equal to the period of their approved stay.

## UNDERSTANDING THE TEMPORARY VISITORS (STUDENT) CATEGORY

There are many different courses available in New Zealand to students from overseas, but it is very important that you first find out whether you are eligible to study in New Zealand. To do this, contact the New Zealand diplomatic or consular office in your home country. If there is no such office, you get the information by writing to the following:

● For primary and secondary schools and technical institutes – International Division, Department of Education, Private Bag, Wellington, New Zealand.

● If you wish to enquire about technical institutions, universities and schools, you can either contact the Ministry of Education, International Division, Private Bag, Wellington, New Zealand, Tel: 64-4-473 5544 or Fax: 64-4-499 1327, or the institution of your choice.

Anyone who wishes to study at a New Zealand educational institution or come to New Zealand for training of any kind *must* apply for a student visa unless the course is for three months or less.

A visas gives you the length of stay (up to a maximum of four years) which will be shown in your student permit. It will also specify:

● the course of study you may undertake

● the name and location of the institution at which you may study.

To apply for a student visa, in addition to the standard visa requirements you will need to supply evidence of your acceptance into an approved course of study or training in New Zealand, together with evidence of payment of, or exemption from, tuition fees. All letters of acceptance must show the length of your course. Your visa will normally be good for a single journey only, if your course of study is less than six months. If you are studying for a longer period, however, you may be able to use your student visa for as many journeys in and out of New Zealand as you wish while the visa is current. This is called a multiple entry visa.

## UNDERSTANDING THE LONG TERM BUSINESS CATEGORY

This is a specific visa/permit established to cater for potential migrants to apply for residence under the Entrepreneur category, to establish a business in New Zealand, but who do not wish to live permanently in New Zealand. Successful applicants for a business visa would be granted a work visa for up to three years.

### Summary of requirements
An applicant for a work (long term business) visa/permit must:

(a) have a satisfactory business proposal plan; *and*

(b) have, in addition to investment capital, sufficient funds for their maintenance and accommodation and that of any non-principal applicants; *and*

(c) have health and character requirements; *and*

(d) satisfy the business immigration specialist that they are genuinely interested in establishing a business in New Zealand.

### Definition of business proposal plan
A business plan is a proposal to establish a specific business in New Zealand and must be supported by appropriate documentation. The proposal form covers the following:

- an outline of the proposed business and of its viability
- financial information (forecasts and financing options)
- the business experience of the applicant
- the applicant's knowledge of the New Zealand market

- other viability factors (including English language).

## UNDERSTANDING THE TEMPORARY VISITORS (TEMPORARY WORKERS) CATEGORY

Anyone who secures a job *before* arriving in New Zealand or intends to come into New Zealand to work, *must* apply for a work visa. This is necessary even if you are from a country which has a visa-waiver arrangement with New Zealand. *Do not* make final arrangements for your departure until you have been advised *in writing* that you application has been approved.

The period of time you are allowed to stay in New Zealand will be written on the visa, and later on the permit. A visa may also limit:

- the kind of work you may do
- the place where you may work
- the person or organisation you may work for.

Work visas can be issued for one journey or multiple journeys to New Zealand. If you intend to travel overseas during the time you are in New Zealand, ask for a multiple-entry visa when you make your application and explain why you need it.

## APPLYING FOR WORK PERMITS

As the purpose of a work permit is to enable employers to fill short-term skills shortages, all applications will be tested against the New Zealand labour market in the following ways:

- by the prospective employer, who must supply evidence in each case that the position offered to an overseas worker cannot be filled locally ('case made' basis); *and/or*
- by the New Zealand Immigration Service officer, both in New Zealand and overseas, which will check an offer of employment through the New Zealand Employment Service.

Normally, unskilled applicants will be refused visas or permits.

If you obtain a work visa *before* you travel to New Zealand, your work permit will be granted for the time given in your contract –

from one day up to a maximum of three years.

If you obtain a visitor's permit on arrival in New Zealand, and then subsequently apply for a work permit, that permit would normally allow you to remain in New Zealand for a total stay of up to six months (the normal maximum visit period).

If you receive a student permit on arrival in New Zealand, a work permit (or a variation of the conditions of your student permit) may be granted. This will enable you to gain practical experience on completion of a three-year course of study, or over the summer vacation. You may not work unless you are granted permission to do so by the New Zealand Immigration Service.

## APPLYING FOR A VISITOR'S VISA

Visitors may come to New Zealand in the following categories:

- as tourists
- for business talks
- to see friends or relatives
- to play sport or perform in cultural events (without pay)
- for medical treatment or medical consultation
- on long term business visas.

To travel to New Zealand you will need a visitor's visa which must be obtained before you leave home. There are exceptions to this rule and these are:

- an Australian citizen travelling on an Australian passport
- an Australian resident with a current Australian resident return visa
- a citizen of any of the following countries, which have visa-waiver agreements with New Zealand:

(*Note*: You must apply for a visa if you plan to visit for more than the time stated below.)

*For visits up to 30 days*
Citizens of France living in Tahiti or New Caledonia.

*For visits up to three months*
Citizens of Austria, Belgium, Brunei, Canada, Denmark, Finland, France,[1] Germany, Greece, Iceland, Indonesia, Ireland, Italy, Japan, Korea (South), Kiribati, Liechtenstein, Luxembourg, Malaysia, Malta, Monaco, Nauru, Netherlands, Norway, Portugal,[2] Singapore, Spain, Sweden, Switzerland, Thailand, Tuvalu, United States of America.

(*Notes:* 1. French citizens living in France only. 2. Portuguese passport-holders must have the right to live permanently in Portugal.)

*For visits up to six months*
British citizens and other British passport-holders who have evidence of the right to live permanently in the United Kingdom.

If you are a citizen of one of the above stated countries, you can apply for a visitor's permit by completing an arrival card when you arrive in New Zealand. The period of time you are allowed to stay will be written inside your visa and permit, and you are *not* allowed to work in New Zealand. Visas enable you to:

• study or train for a single course of not more than three months

• undergo medical treatment

• take a holiday.

You will need to supply a completed **Application for Visitor's Visa**, fee, passport and a recent passport-size photo. You may also be required to show that you have enough money to support yourself during your stay here, i.e. NZ$1,000 for each person per month or NZ$400 each person per month if your accommodation is already paid, and evidence of this (prepaid hotel vouchers) must be available. Details of your travel arrangements to leave New Zealand must also be shown. If you wish to make more than one journey to New Zealand you should apply for a multiple visa.

## KNOWING ABOUT THE UNITED KINGDOM CITIZENS' WORKING HOLIDAY SCHEME

This scheme was designed to enable British citizens to have a working holiday for twelve months in New Zealand. Until recently the allowance per year was for 500 people. It was announced in November 1995 that the allowance was to be increased to 2,000 people per year. Contact your nearest New Zealand Immigration department for further details.

## PERMANENT MIGRANTS

Under the Immigration Act 1987, every person who wishes to immigrate to New Zealand needs to apply for New Zealand residence. This will entitle you to live, study and work indefinitely in New Zealand. If you wish to leave New Zealand temporarily, you must have a valid New Zealand returning resident's visa in your passport, to ensure your re-entry to New Zealand as a resident.

If you are outside New Zealand when you apply, you should apply for a Residence Visa at an accredited New Zealand consular or diplomatic office. If you are inside New Zealand when you apply, you should apply for a Residence Permit to your nearest New Zealand Immigration Service branch office.

There are two very important and compulsory requirements that you and your accompanying family (if applicable) must meet in order to be granted New Zealand residence. They are that you must be in 'good health' and 'of good character'. In order to prove that you are in good health you are required to provide:

- medical certificates for you and your family, less than three months old at the date that you lodge your application; *and*

- X-ray certificates for you and your family, less than three months old at the date that you lodge your application.

In order to prove that you are 'of good character' everyone of 17 years of age and over must provide:

- police certificates from your country of citizenship

- police certificates from any country you have been in for twelve months or more in the last ten years.

People considered not of good character include people to whom Section 7(1) of the Immigration Act applies:

- persons who have been convicted and sentenced to prison for five years or more, or convicted and sentenced to imprisonment for one year or more during the last ten years
- those whom there is a reason to believe may be associated with criminal groups or who constitute a danger to New Zealand.

## BECOMING A PERMANENT MIGRANT

Migrants will be considered for permanent residence under five major categories. These are:

- General Skills Category
- Business Investor Category
- Entrepreneur Category
- Family Category
- Humanitarian Category.

The *General Skills Category* replaces the former General Category points system with an auto pass mark which ranks applicants on their qualifications, work experience, age and settlement factors. A minimum level of English language ability will also be required.

The *Business Investor Category* will not only test skills and experience, but also require applicants to transfer a fixed amount of capital to New Zealand for a set period of time. A minimum level of English language ability is also required.

Applicants with a genuine relationship with a New Zealand partner, adult child, sibling or parent will be able to apply under the *Family Category.*

The *Humanitarian Category* considers people in exceptionally difficult circumstances who have a close family connection with New Zealand.

The *Entrepreneur Category* has been set up to grant residence to those people who have established a business in New Zealand successfully for a period of two years.

A new category for retirement visas was being considered by the government at the time of updating this book. For more up-to-date information contact the New Zealand Immigration Services.

## BECOMING A PERMANENT MIGRANT – GENERAL SKILLS CATEGORY

The emphasis of the General Skills Category is on assessing the overall human capital of the applicant, with migrants being allocated points for attributes and then periodically ranked (if you score 24 points or less, your application will be declined). Those scoring the higher number of points may be eligible for residence, *provided they satisfy the normal immigration criteria.* Contact the New Zealand Immigration Service for the current pass mark. The main areas tested are detailed below.

### Employability

This relates to offer of employment, age and work experience and is the major element, and will relate to qualifications and work experience. You need to supply original or certified true copies of your qualifications, and evidence that you were employed in your stated occupation for the stated length of time.

The following rules apply:

1. You can only obtain points for *one* qualification.

2. Partially completed qualifications will not be accepted.

3. Your qualification must be of a comparable standard to a New Zealand qualification.

*Note*: In New Zealand there are certain occupations for which you must have membership of and/or registration with a professional or industrial organisation. Some samples of such occupations are:

| | |
|---|---|
| Dental technicians | Electricians |
| Lawyers | Medical personnel |
| Optometrists | Pharmacists |
| Plumbers and gas-fitters | Veterinarians |

*Statutory registration*
Where applicable, professional registration will be required before an applicant qualifies for points equivalent to their qualifications. Evidence of registration must be available to the Immigration Service at the time an application is assessed for points. If you are registered this will assist the New Zealand Immigration Service in making an accurate assessment of your qualification.

## Qualifications
The points you can be allocated are as follows:

| | |
|---|---|
| Any equivalent to a New Zealand base degree, trade or three-year diploma/certificate | 10 points |
| New Zealand advanced trade or professional qualification – minimum one year training, study or work experience | 11 points |
| New Zealand Masters or better | 12 points |

*Applicants must reach a 10 point minimum requirement.*

**How many points will you be claiming for qualifications?** ☐ **points**

## New Zealand qualifications
You can be allocated an extra point if you have completed a qualification in New Zealand for which you have been, or could have been, awarded qualification points. This would not be available if you received New Zealand Overseas Development Assistance (NZODA) scholarship assistance to complete the New Zealand qualification. A New Zealand qualification is defined as a qualification conferred by a New Zealand institute, with at least half the course time undertaken in attendance at the institute in New Zealand.

## Work experience
Points are allocated on the basis of work experience for 30 hours or more per week. Work experience for less may be awarded points on a pro rata basis. You can only claim a maximum of 10 points. You must score a minimum of one point. If you hold a New Zealand qualification which is eligible and you did not receive NZODA assistance, you are not required to score one point under this classification. If you are not awarded points for a job offer then only your work experience relevant to your qualifications will count for points. If you are awarded points for a job offer then your work experience does not have to be relevant to your qualification to count for points. You can claim one point for every two complete year's work experience.

All work experience must be sound. It is not sound if it was gained before 20 years of age, unless it was after the qualification for which points are awarded; if it was gained during compulsory military or community service, unless it is relevant to the qualification for which points are awarded; or of such a low standard as to lead to your dismissal.

Points are scored as follows:

| | |
|---|---|
| 2 years | 1 point |
| 4 years | 2 points |
| 6 years | 3 points |
| 8 years | 4 points |
| 10 years | 5 points |
| 12 years | 6 points |
| 14 years | 7 points |
| 16 years | 8 points |
| 18 years | 9 points |
| 20 years | 10 points |

**How many points will you be claiming for work experience?**                    ☐ **point(s)**

## Job offer

You can be allocated a maximum of 5 points if you receive a job offer from a New Zealand employer that is:

- for ongoing employment by a single employer, *and*
- for full-time employment, *and*
- current at the time of application.

The employment must be permanent, or for a term of at least twelve months with an option of further terms after that. Positions of self employment, or payment by commission and/or retainer are not acceptable. You must obtain full registration if this is required by law to take up the offer of employment. If you are claiming points for a qualification in an occupation for which registration is required by law in New Zealand, you must provide an offer of employment in an occupation that does not require registration and is assessed as relevant to the qualification for which points are claimed. An offer of employment is considered to be relevant to the applicant's qualification if the qualification is an important factor in being able to obtain, continue or advance in the job offered; or the offer of employment is part of a career path which had advanced progressively from the immediate area in which you are qualified.

## Age

You can be allocated points for your age. Normally you can only claim points for the age that you are at the time that you lodge your application for residence. However, if you turn 25 years while your application is being processed your points for age can be increased.

*Note:*
If you are 56 years of age or over, your application for residence cannot be approved under the General Skills category.

Points for age will be allocated as follows:

| | |
|---|---|
| 18–24 years | 8 points |
| 25–29 years | 10 points |
| 30–34 years | 8 points |
| 35–39 years | 6 points |
| 40–44 years | 4 points |
| 45–49 years | 2 points |
| 50–55 years | 0 points |

**How many points will you be claiming for age?**  ☐ **points**

### Settlement factors
You can be awarded points for factors which will assist you in settling in New Zealand. The maximum number of points you can score under this section is 7.

### Settlement funds
You can be allocated points for settlement funds (i.e. cash, shares, stocks and any other assets). These funds must be transferred to New Zealand before residence will be granted and they must be free of debt. You have six months from the date of approval in principle to transfer your funds.

You can be allocated points if the funds are owned wholly by the principal applicant or spouse or owned jointly by the principal applicant and spouse. You can only score a maximum of 2 points.

Points can be scored as follows:

| | |
|---|---|
| NZ$100,000 | 1 point |
| NZ$200,000 | 2 points |

**How many points will you be claiming for settlement funds?**  ☐ **point(s)**

## Spouse or partner's qualifications

You can be allocated a maximum of 2 points for your spouse's fully completed qualification if it is comparable to a New Zealand standard. The comparable New Zealand standard will be determined by the New Zealand Immigration Service or the New Zealand Qualifications Authority.

*Note:*
- Your spouse can only be allocated points for either one qualification or a series of qualifications (accepted as being comparable to one New Zealand qualification).
- Partially completed qualifications will not be accepted.

Points are scored as follows:

| | |
|---|---|
| Degree, diploma or trade certificate of a minimum of 3 years duration | 1 point |
| Advanced qualification, masters degree or higher of a minimum of 4 years duration | 2 points |

**How many points will you be claiming for your spouse's qualification?**    ☐ **point(s)**

## New Zealand work experience

You can score a maximum of 2 points for work experience gained lawfully in New Zealand. You can be allocated points for New Zealand work experience under both this section and the Work Experience section. The rules about relevance and soundness found under Work Experience apply to New Zealand work experience.

Points are allocated on the basis of work experience for 30 hours or more per week. Work experience for less than 30 hours per week may be awarded points on a pro rata basis. You can claim 1 point for each complete year of work experience.

**How many points will you be claiming for New Zealand work experience?**    ☐ **point(s)**

## Family sponsorship

You can be allocated points for a family sponsor. Your family sponsor must be:

- 17 years and over; *and*
- a New Zealand citizen or resident; *and*
- have been lawfully and permanently living in New Zealand for at least three years; *and*
- a parent, brother, sister or child of the principal applicant or the principal applicant's spouse.

If your family member undertakes to be your sponsor, they are responsible for:

- providing information and advice about settling in New Zealand; *and*
- if necessary, ensuring accommodation is available to you for up to 12 months from your date of arrival in New Zealand.

They must complete the New Zealand Immigration Service Sponsorship Form and present it to a New Zealand Immigration Service branch office to have it endorsed. If you meet the requirements, you can score a maximum of 3 points for family sponsorship.

**What are the total points you wish to claim
under the General Skills Category?** ☐ **point(s)**

**Migrant levy**
A migrant is levied on all successful principal applicants and accompanying family members in the General Skills and Business Investor categories. The migrant levy is NZ$180 for each person included in an application, up to a maximum of NZ$720 for each application. The migrant levy must be paid before residence is granted. Outside New Zealand the levy is usually paid in local currency.

**Settlement information fee**
A settlement information fee applies to all successful principal or sole applicants except citizens of Samoa and refugees. The fee is NZ$90 and must be paid before residence is granted. Outside New Zealand, the fee is usually paid in local currency.

## BECOMING A PERMANENT MIGRANT (BUSINESS INVESTOR CATEGORY)

The aim of the Business Investor Category is to ensure that high-quality migrants with excellent, proven business skills and experience, who can foster international linkages, gain entry to New Zealand. Generally, they are also expected to invest business funds in New Zealand. You will be granted residence under the Business Investor Category if you score enough points to meet the pass mark (*if you score 11 points or less, your application will be declined*) and you meet the compulsory requirements. The pass mark is recalculated for the start of each week. Contact the New Zealand Immigration Service for the current pass mark. Website: *http://www.immigration.govt.nz*

### English language ability

All principal applicants for residence under the Business Investor Category must have an acceptable standard of English language ability. You must therefore produce evidence of either:

- having an English language background; *or*

- that you have met 'band level 5' in each of the 4 components of the International English Language Testing System (IELTS).

You may request IELTS information from the New Zealand Immigration Service.

### Human and investment capital factors – business experience

You can be allocated points for the business experience you have gained. Business experience is defined as having:

- a minimum of two years owning or managing a lawful business enterprise or senior management experience in a lawful business enterprise.

Points are allocated on the basis of business experience of 30 hours or more per week. Business experience for less than 30 hours per week may be awarded points on a pro rata basis:

- e.g. business experience of 15 hours per week for eight years would equate to four years of business experience for 30 hours per week and would attract 1 point.

You can claim 1 point for each completed four-year period of business experience.

*Note:*
You can only claim a maximum of 5 points under the Business Experience section.

Points are scored as follows:

| | |
|---|---|
| 4 years | 1 point |
| 8 years | 2 points |
| 12 years | 3 points |
| 16 years | 4 points |
| 20 years or more | 5 points |

**How many points will you be claiming
for business experience?** ☐ **point(s)**

### Qualifications

You can be allocated points for a fully completed qualification that is comparable to a New Zealand standard. The comparable New Zealand standard will be determined by the New Zealand Immigration Service or the New Zealand Qualifications Authority.

*Note:*
- You can only be allocated points for either one qualification or a series of qualifications (accepted as being comparable to one New Zealand qualification).
- Partially completed qualifications will not be accepted.
- Where registration is required by law in New Zealand, applicants must gain registration before points will be awarded.
- The qualification must be related to the business experience that you are to be allocated points for.

Points are scored as follows:

| | |
|---|---|
| Base qualification | 1 point |
| Advanced qualification, masters degree or higher | 2 points |

**How many points will you be claiming
for qualifications?** ☐ **point(s)**

## Accumulated earnings funds

You can be allocated a maximum of 10 points for accumulated earnings funds and assets that:

- were earned through your business experience in a lawful business enterprise; *and*
- will be invested in New Zealand for two years in an investment capable of providing a commercial return.

*Note:*

- You can only be allocated points if the funds are owned wholly by the principal applicant or jointly with the principal applicant's spouse.
- You need not transfer your money to New Zealand until your application has been approved in principle.

Points are scored as follows:

| NZ$ | |
| --- | --- |
| 750,000 | 1 point |
| 1,000,000 | 2 points |
| 1,250,000 | 3 points |
| 1,500,000 | 4 points |
| 1,750,000 | 5 points |
| 2,000,000 | 6 points |
| 2,250,000 | 7 points |
| 2,500,000 | 8 points |
| 2,750,000 | 9 points |
| 3,000,000 | 10 points |

**How many points will you be claiming
for accumulated earnings funds?** ☐ **point(s)**

## Direct investment funds

Some, or all, accumulated earnings funds may be nominated as direct investment funds. Additional points may be awarded for any amount nominated as both accumulated earnings funds and direct investment funds.

Direct investment funds are defined as funds used to acquire a

significant influence in the management of an enterprise in New Zealand undertaking bona fide trading activities:
A significant influence is defined as:

1. ownership of 25 per cent or more of the business; *and*

2. an active role in the management of the business.

Direct investment funds must remain in an acceptable investment in New Zealand for a two-year period.

*Note:*
- You can only be allocated points if the funds are owned wholly by the principal applicant or jointly with the principal applicant's spouse.
- You need not transfer your money to New Zealand until your application has been approved in principle.

Points are scored as follows:

| | |
|---|---|
| NZ$ 750,000 | 3 points |
| NZ$ 1,250,000 | 4 points |
| NZ$ 1,750,000 | 5 points |

**How many points will you be claiming
for direct investment funds?**                    ☐ **points**

## Age

You can be allocated points for your age. However, if you are between 55 and 64 years you will be deducted points as listed in the following chart. If you are 65 years of age and over, your application cannot be approved under the Business Investor Category.

Points are scored as follows:

| | |
|---|---|
| 25–29 years | 10 points |
| 30–34 years | 8 points |
| 35–39 years | 6 points |
| 40–44 years | 4 points |
| 45–49 years | 2 points |
| 50–54 years | 0 points |
| 55–59 years | − 2 points |
| 60–64 years | − 4 points |

**How many points will you be claiming for age?**    ☐ **points**

## Settlement factors
You can be awarded points for factors which will assist you in settling in New Zealand. The maximum number of points you will be awarded under this section is 7.

## Settlement funds
You can be allocated points for settlement funds (i.e. cash, shares, stock and any other assets). These funds must be transferred to New Zealand before residence will be granted and must be free of debt.

*Note:*
- You can be allocated points if the funds are owned wholly by either the principal applicant or spouse or owned jointly by the principal applicant and spouse.
- You can claim a maximum of two points.
- You need not transfer your funds to New Zealand until your application has been approved in principle.

Points are scored as follows:

| | |
|---|---|
| NZ$100,000 | 1 point |
| NZ$200,000 | 2 points |

**How many points will you be claiming for settlements funds?**      ☐ **point(s)**

## Spouse or partner's qualifications
You can be allocated points for your spouse's fully completed qualification if it is comparable to a New Zealand standard. The comparable New Zealand standard will be determined by the New Zealand Immigration Service or the New Zealand Qualifications Authority. The comparability rules are the same as for the principal applicant.

Points are scored as follows:

| | |
|---|---|
| Base qualification | 1 point |
| Advanced qualification, masters degree or higher | 2 points |

**How many points will you be claiming for your spouse or partner's qualification?**      ☐ **point(s)**

## New Zealand business experience

You can score points for lawful business experience that you have gained in New Zealand as:

- the owner and manager of a business; *or*

- a senior manager in a business.

Points are allocated on the basis of business experience of 30 hours or more per week. Business experience for less than 30 hours per week may be awarded points on a pro rata basis:

- e.g. business experience of 15 hours per week for two years would equate to one year of business experience for 30 hours per week and would attract 1 point.

You can claim 1 point for each complete year of New Zealand business experience, up to a maximum of 2 points.

Points are scored as follows:

| | |
|---|---|
| 1 year | 1 point |
| 2 years | 2 points |

**How many points will you be claiming
for New Zealand business experience?**        ☐ **point(s)**

## Family sponsorship

You can be allocated 3 points for family sponsorship. Your family sponsor must be:

- over 17 years; *and*

- a New Zealand citizen or resident; *and*

- residing in New Zealand for at least 3 years; *and*

- a parent, brother, sister or child of the principal applicant.

If your family member undertakes to be your sponsor, they are responsible for:

- providing information and advice about settling in New Zealand; *and*

• if necessary, ensuring accommodation is available to you for up to 12 months from your date of arrival in New Zealand.

They must complete the New Zealand Immigration Service Sponsorship Form and present it to the New Zealand Immigration Service branch office to have it endorsed.

**How many points will you be claiming for family sponsorship?**  ☐ **point(s)**

**What are the total points you wish to claim under the Business Investor Category?**  ☐ **points**

## Transfer of funds

If you gain a points pass, you will be required to transfer your funds to New Zealand.

If you were awarded points for direct investment funds you can apply for a twelve-month work visa. This allows you twelve months in which to decide on how you want to invest your funds in New Zealand. It does not allow you to enter into salaried employment in New Zealand. Once you have shown that you have an acceptable investment, you will be granted residence. You also have twelve months to transfer your settlement funds.

If you were awarded points for accumulated earnings funds but not direct investment funds, you will be given six months from the date of approval in which to transfer your funds (including investment funds). If you show that you have made an acceptable investment of your accumulated earnings funds, you will be granted conditional residence.

## Two-year investment period

Under the Business Investor Category, your residence in new Zealand will be subject to requirements. You will be required to retain your funds in an acceptable investment for a period of two years. If you have met these requirements at the end of two years, you will be granted residence without requirements. If you do not meet the requirements, your residence may be revoked and you may be required to leave New Zealand.

## BECOMING A PERMANENT MIGRANT (ENTREPRENEUR CATEGORY)

The Entrepreneur Category has been set up to grant residence to those people who have established a business in New Zealand successfully for a period of two years. An applicant will be considered to have successfully established a business in New Zealand if:

- they have established or purchased, or made a substantial investment in a business operating in New Zealand, *and*

- the business has been established for at least two years; *and*

- the applicant has been self-employed in New Zealand in that business for at least two years.

The business may be deemed as benefiting New Zealand if it promotes New Zealand's economic growth through:

- increased competition
- introduction of new technology, management or technical skills
- introduction of new products or services
- development of new export markets or increased market access
- creation of new job opportunities
- the revitalising of an existing business.

In addition to this, all applicants must meet health, character and English language requirements.

### Description of the business

Applicants are required to give details of their business. Information provided should address the following points:

- a description of the business
- the industry the business operates in
- the customers, suppliers and distribution network of the business; *and*
- the business benefits to New Zealand.

For further information contact your nearest New Zealand Immigration Service office, or website: http://www.immigration.govt.nz/forms/

## BECOMING A PERMANENT MIGRANT (FAMILY CATEGORY)

This category covers three situations:

● marriage to a New Zealand citizen or resident

● de facto/homosexual relationship with a citizen or resident

● parents, dependent children, and single adult brothers, sisters, and children.

### Spouses

A legally married spouse of a New Zealand resident or citizen may qualify for residence. Approval is not automatic, and an interview with both partners may be held before residence is granted.

### Partners

De facto or homosexual partners of New Zealand citizens or residents may be considered for residence. Once again, approval is not automatic, and an interview with both partners may be held. The couple will need to show they are living together in a stable, lasting relationship. The relationship must be of at least two years duration in the case of a de facto couple, and four years if the relationship is a homosexual relationship.

### Parents, siblings, children

If you are a parent, you are eligible to be reunited with your adult children in New Zealand (provided all your adult children are living permanently outside your home country, or you have an equal or greater number of adult children lawfully permanently resident in New Zealand than anywhere else). Limited provisions exist for parents with dependent children. Single adult brothers, sisters and children of New Zealand citizens or residents (including persons who are divorced or widowed) are eligible for residence, provided they have no children and have no immediate family in their home country.

### Sponsors

If you are applying under family reunification, you will need a sponsor or support from the New Zealand based relative for at least 24 months.

## Dependent children

Unmarried dependent children under 19 are eligible for residence if they:

- are joining their parent(s) in New Zealand
- have no children of their own
- were declared in their parents' application for residence, and provided their parents are lawfully and permanently living in New Zealand
- were born or adopted before their parents applied for residence, and they were declared on their parents' application for residence; or they were born after their parents applied for residence; or they were adopted by their parents as a result of a New Zealand adoption or an overseas adoption recognised under New Zealand law

Children with parents who are separated or divorced, must provide evidence that the custody or visitation rights of a parent living outside New Zealand would not be breached by the child coming to New Zealand.

## BECOMING A PERMANENT MIGRANT (HUMANITARIAN CATEGORY)

This category provides for the entry into New Zealand of people whose circumstances are exceptionally difficult.

The applicant must have at least one close relative who is a New Zealand citizen or resident, and who supports the application.

Applicants will be assessed under the following criteria:

- their circumstances must be such that they, or a New Zealand party, is suffering serious physical or emotional harm; *and*
- their application is supported by a close family member who is a New Zealand citizen or resident; *and*
- they produce evidence to show why their situation can only be resolved by their being granted residence in New Zealand; *and*
- it would not be contrary to the public interest to allow the applicants to reside in New Zealand.

Your family sponsor must be aged 17 years or over. Either a New Zealand citizen or the holder of a New Zealand residence permit not subject to requirements under Section 18A of the Immigration Act 1986, and you or your spouse's or partner's parent, adult sibling, adult child, aunt, uncle, nephew, niece, grandparent or a person who has lived with and been part of your family for many years. Your sponsors will be responsible for ensuring accommodation is available to you for at least your first 24 months as a resident in New Zealand.

To get full details about applying for residence, request a residence application pack from your nearest New Zealand Immigration Office.

(*Information source*: New Zealand Immigration Service.)

## CASE STUDIES

### Simon missed out, but...
Simon applied to New Zealand House in London for the United Kingdom Citizens' Working Holiday Scheme work visa hoping to be lucky enough to get a visa. Unfortunately he failed in the annual ballot. Simon decided that he would travel to New Zealand via America, where he worked for several months.

He arrived in New Zealand on a six-month visitor's permit and looked around for employment to help pay for his holiday. As Simon was a very well qualified landscape architect he was able to find a job immediately because the firm had been advertising in New Zealand for staff and had not received much response. Because of this and with the help of his new employer he was able to get a work permit for six months. Simon is enjoying his time in New Zealand and has found that the landscape profession there is very small and reasonably buoyant. He knows that he could return to New Zealand after this short visit, and find work immediately, because of the contacts he has been able to make.

### Heather was one of the lucky ones
Heather had always wanted to visit New Zealand. She found out about the working holiday scheme, applied, and was lucky enough to be allowed into New Zealand to work for a year. Heather had only just finished her degree in French and EU Studies, and knew that she would be unlikely to find a job in her new field, so she prepared herself by taking a crash course in word processing.

As she wanted to explore the country as much as possible, she didn't want work that would take up her weekends, so she signed up with a personnel consultancy firm, and was able to get temping assignments as a receptionist for several large organisations. Although Heather has enjoyed discovering New Zealand she feels that it would never replace the UK for her.

### Jenny and Sean wanted to study and work

Jenny and Sean had been able to get student visas for their three years study and completed their degree. They wanted to find work for the summer and decided that they would like to see more of New Zealand before they returned to England. They found summer jobs picking fruit, and drifted around the countryside working whenever they could. Their lifestyle was slow and lazy compared with their three years of study, and the days just passed by. One day Jenny was checking through her documents and found to her dismay that their student visas had expired. They quickly contacted the nearest Immigration department, and found that not only had they been working in New Zealand with expired study visas, they had also been working illegally because they should have contacted the Immigration Service to arrange for work permits. They stay was cut short because they were told they must leave New Zealand immediately.

### POINTS FOR DISCUSSION

1. Could you afford to come and experience New Zealand on a year's working holiday before making firm plans to stay permanently?

2. If you were unable to get permanent status in New Zealand could you consider living half the year in your homeland and spending the other half of the year in New Zealand?

3. If you were studying in a New Zealand university, would you be able to support your stay without working?

# 4

## Understanding Employment Conditions and Law

### SIGNING A CONTRACT

The following is a summary of the provisions of the Contracts Act 1991:

This Act removes monopolies over coverage and bargaining and gives employees the right to decide whether or not they wish to belong to an employees' organisation, such as a union, and the right to choose who, if anybody, they want to represent them. It aims to encourage bargaining outcomes that are relevant to the workplace and enables employers to negotiate either individual or collective employment contracts directly.

In particular the Act provides for:

*Freedom of association and voluntary membership of employees' organisations* – employees can determine for themselves whether or not they wish to join any form of employees' organisation, such as a union, and they are protected from undue influence in making that decision. No one, including employers, is able to compel any employee to join a union or to stop those who want to join from doing so.

*Bargaining arrangements* – the nature of bargaining arrangements is negotiable with employers or their representative. In particular:

- Every employer has an employment contract with every employee, either as an individual contract or as a collective contract.

- Employees and employers have the right to authorise another person, group or organisation to represent them in negotiations for an employment contract.

- Representatives must establish their authority to represent their employee or employer client and that authority must be recognised by the other party.

- Anybody may act as a representative, provided they have not been convicted of an offence punishable by five years or more in prison, within the last 20 years.

- Employees are required to formulate, together with their bargaining agent, an agreed procedure for the ratification of any settlement of a collective contract negotiated by the representative.

- Authorised representatives have rights of access to the workplace to assist the process of negotiation at any reasonable time.

- Authorised representatives may become party to an employment contract when the employer, employees and representative concerned all agree.

The bargaining arrangements give employers and employees the freedom to negotiate about what type of contract they want, and about the content of the contract, which may include any matter they choose. Thus a variety of contractual arrangements is possible, including individual or collective contracts and contracts which cover a single employer or a number of employers. Collective contracts will bind only those who agree to be included. The parties may agree to include a clause in a collective contract that new employees are permitted to join the contract, with the agreement of the new employee at the time the employment commences.

## JOINING A UNION

A new New Zealand government (Labour/Alliance) and a new President of the Council of Trade Unions (CTU), means that the falling membership of the CTU could be halted and improved on.

Mr Ross Wilson, the new President, said recently that top of his priority list was to bring all New Zealand's unions together into a single organisation. The CTU has a strength of 204,476 workers in 19 unions.

The new government has stated its intentions to restore the union's power which has steadily diminished since the Employment

Contracts Act was introduced in 1991, which stated that workers were no longer forced to join unions.

## HANDLING A PERSONAL GRIEVANCE

An employee may claim a personal grievance against an employer for unjustifiable dismissal, other unjustifiable action by the employer, discrimination, sexual harassment, and duress in relation to membership or non-membership of an employees' organisation. All employment contracts must contain an effective procedure for the settlement of personal grievances. This can be the standard procedure as set out in the First Schedule to the Contracts Act 1991, or another procedure not inconsistent with the standard one. The application of the procedures is not able to be frustrated by the deliberate lack of co-operation on the part of any person. Depending on the circumstances of each case, the remedy in the case of a proven grievance can include reimbursement for lost wages, reinstatement, and compensation for humiliation, loss of dignity and injury to feelings.

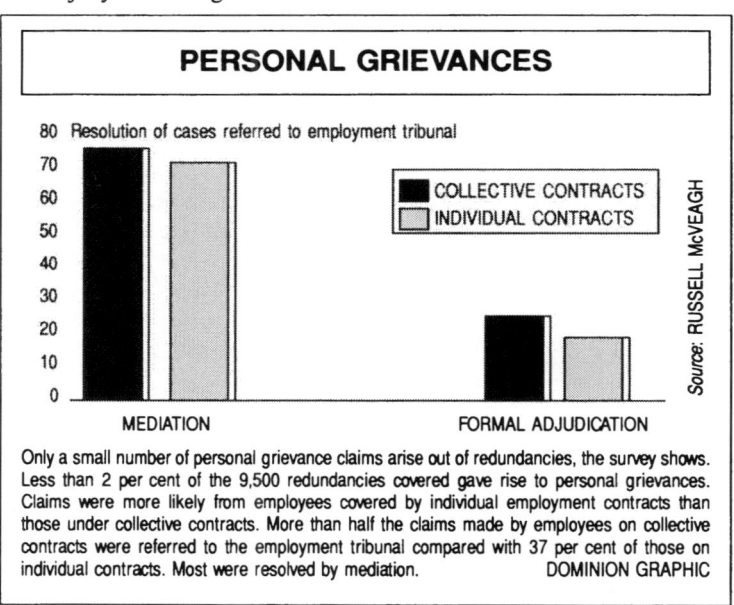

**PERSONAL GRIEVANCES**

Resolution of cases referred to employment tribunal

◼ COLLECTIVE CONTRACTS
▨ INDIVIDUAL CONTRACTS

MEDIATION          FORMAL ADJUDICATION

*Source:* RUSSELL McVEAGH

Only a small number of personal grievance claims arise out of redundancies, the survey shows. Less than 2 per cent of the 9,500 redundancies covered gave rise to personal grievances. Claims were more likely from employees covered by individual employment contracts than those under collective contracts. More than half the claims made by employees on collective contracts were referred to the employment tribunal compared with 37 per cent of those on individual contracts. Most were resolved by mediation.          DOMINION GRAPHIC

Fig. 3. Personal grievance claims.

## KNOWING YOUR RIGHTS

Certain other provisions, known as the Minimum Code of Employment, provide statutory minimum entitlements which apply to all employees. These include:

- Statutory minimum wage at two levels – an adult minimum wage applying to employees aged 20 and over, and a youth minimum wage applying to people age 16 to 19.
- Protection from unlawful deductions from wages.
- 11 paid public holidays where the holiday would otherwise be a working day.
- Three weeks paid annual leave after 12 months employment.
- Five days special leave after six months employment.
- Parental leave and employment protection.
- Equal pay for men and women.
- Access to procedures for resolving personal grievances and disputes.

## TAKING MATERNITY LEAVE

A woman is entitled to up to 14 weeks maternity leave, of which up to six weeks may be taken before the birth or, if agreed by the employer, a period before the adoption of a child under five years. Employers may not dismiss an employee for being pregnant or for applying for parental leave. Employees who are dismissed or given notice of dismissal for either of these reasons have a special right to go directly to the Employment Tribunal and ask for a temporary order to give them their job back, or cancel the notice of dismissal.

## CASE STUDIES

### Jackie didn't want to negotiate

Jackie had been employed for two years. She had been overlooked at the assessment time the previous year and felt she couldn't face up to complaining or negotiating with her very forceful employer for a salary increase. She had joined the PSA (New Zealand Public Service Association) some months earlier and upon enquiring she found that they were able to negotiate a fair wage increase for her.

They were also able to advise her of the market fluctuations in salary increases for her type of work. This was a great relief for Jackie as she knew she wouldn't be able to do it alone.

## Colin deals with discrimination

Colin who was aged 49 years felt that he was being overlooked in the advancement arena. Although his work had been stated to be satisfactory there was no sign of advancement. After a visit to the union representative he was informed that it was possible take a 'personal grievance' case in the form of 'age discrimination'. Colin was successful and was promoted to project manager within two months.

## David is forced to leave

David had been working for the firm of accountants for over two years. A new administration manager joined the organisation and immediately took a dislike to him. She inferred that he wasn't working to full capacity, and only worked on the jobs that he felt suited him. David was astounded, he had always worked hard, in fact his fellow workmates used to comment on this. He finally had an interview with one of the partners and the administration manager, and found that they had definitely made up a case against his dismissal. David was so indignant at the way it was worded that he asked them if they were firing him. The administration manager then asked him if two weeks' notice would be suitable. David said that he preferred to leave there and then. He consulted with the union who agreed that he had a case of unfair dismissal. A lawyer was hired and David was awarded $7,000, and the firm were told they had to re-hire him. David chose to find another job.

## POINTS FOR DISCUSSION

1. The Minimum Wage Act 1983 states that *unless* the parties agree otherwise, every employment contract under the Employment Contracts Act shall fix the working week at not more than 40 hours, exclusive of overtime. When signing a contract how would you ensure that your hours are clearly defined, and what overtime you will be entitled to?

2. Would you feel that you needed the representation that joining a union would give you?

3. Are you able to negotiate and understand all the relevant points that cover your employment, before signing a contract?

# 5

## Your Workplace Environment

### FINDING YOUR NICHE

The old adage 'when in Rome do as the Romans do' applies in New Zealand, as it does in most places in the world.

Kiwis like to feel that new migrants fall in love with their country as soon as they set foot there. A word of advice – the last thing kiwis like to hear is 'how it is done at home, in England'. Don't complain at the kiwi differences, enjoy them!

### SMOKEFREE

Tobacco products consumption per adult in 1993 fell 2 per cent below the 1992 level to 1,579 cigarette equivalents per adult, among the lowest for developed countries. Doorstep surveys of 10,000 persons during 1992 showed that 27 per cent of adults (28 per cent of men and 26 per cent of women) and 30 per cent of 15–24-year-olds regularly smoked either manufactured or hand-rolled cigarettes.

Restaurants endeavour to limit smokers to a small area while cinemas and theatres are smokefree and so are all internal flights within New Zealand and all public transport systems. Most professional organisations prefer their employees not to smoke, and most office buildings are smokefree. If you happen to pass by at around 10.00 a.m., lunchtime or 3.00 p.m., you may well see groups of smokers congregated outside buildings for that life-giving puff. Some organisations will even prefer not to employ smokers, and the smokers who do work for them, especially in government departments, may be encouraged to quit the habit.

## WORKING WITH COMPUTERS

Most offices are highly computerised with Microsoft 6 being the most popular program because of its versatile office package, e.g. Schedulers for keeping up with diaries, and Email for internal communications around organisations in the same building and in other branches.

Occupational Strain Syndrome (OSS) is a commonplace word among computer users, and most operators know of the necessary breaks and exercises that are recommended and the need for ergonomically correct desks.

## COPING WITH ACCIDENTS

A comprehensive system of accident rehabilitation and compensation insurance is provided for all New Zealanders under the Accident Rehabilitation and Compensation Insurance Act 1992. The Act has an emphasis on injury prevention, rehabilitation, risk management and compensation. It specifically acknowledges that risk management and rehabilitation are facets of injury and compensation cost control and that injury prevention, rehabilitation, risk management and compensation strategies need to be integrated.

Accident Rehabilitation and Compensation Insurance Corporation (ACC) is a form of compulsory insurance where the community as a whole, through the premiums paid, accepts responsibility for the accidents which inevitably afflict a proportion of its members. When you are employed a proportion of the levy is paid by your employer and a proportion by you, the employee.

*Note*: It is not possible in New Zealand for an individual to sue for personal injury. Compensation may be sought through the ACC scheme.

## KEEPING SAFE AND HEALTHY

The Occupational Safety and Health Service is one of the five services to industry maintained by the Department of Labour. It is the primary authority responsible for setting occupational safety and health standards for all industries.

The role of the Occupational Safety and Health Service is to minimise the economic and social cost of workplace illness and injury. This involves administering and enforcing the Health and Safety in Employment Act 1992, developing occupational safety and health policy and providing health services to industry.

The service has extensive direct involvement with industry. It employs inspection staff with specific industry experience, as well as medical, engineering, scientific and technical personnel to provide advisory services. In 1993–94 its 280 staff reported over 120,000 intervention activities in workplaces. Of these, approximately 60 per cent of the total recorded activities related to the enforcement of legislation, while 40 per cent comprised promotional and non-enforcement activities.

## CASE STUDIES

### Sue is afflicted by OSS
Sue was a very fast word processing operator. She was regularly given large contracts to reformulate which required constant and repetitive key movements. In her anxiety to be regarded as the 'best' she ignored all the cautions, recommendations and the all-telling first signs of aches in her hands and shoulders and neck.

Very soon Sue couldn't move her hands comfortably, and was seen to be continually taking pain-killers. She wouldn't complain to her boss because she wanted to seem superhuman and irreplaceable. Eventually she had to see her doctor who immediately told her to stop working and she had to rest her arms and hands for a month. Her boss realised he had asked too much of her, but she had to endure pain before there was any recognition of responsibility.

### Barbara and John dine out
Barbara and John had settled into New Zealand very quickly, and in the first month of arriving there they were introduced to a group of people with similar interests. An evening was planned for a meal out at a small intimate restaurant. Barbara was pleased to be going out and meeting people once more, as she had experienced severe home sickness since leaving England. The evening was very relaxing and she was enjoying learning about the experiences of their new found friends. John took out his cigarettes and began to light up when the coffee arrived. Barbara whispered to him that she thought it was a non-smoking restaurant. He took no notice of her, although the people in the group were giving him strange looks. Finally, the owner

came to their table and whispered discretely to John that it was a non-smoking eating place. John looked embarrassed and quickly put out his cigarette.

## Dennis works too hard

Dennis worked in the main office of a large organisation and he was required to photocopy and staple large mail-outs on a regular basis. He thought that the work was easy, and used to joke about getting paid for stuffing envelopes. After an extremely large mail-out, and several hours of stapling papers together, he found that he couldn't lift his right arm. The doctor diagnosed severe strain and said he was a typical victim of occupational strain syndrome. Dennis found that he was unable to use his arm at all. He was put on sickness benefit, and was unable to work again for several months. When he returned to work he made sure that his work was interspersed with different activities so that he was not afflicted again.

## POINTS FOR DISCUSSION

1. In some cases, when it is defined in the job application, you may find that a smoker is not wanted in a workforce that is totally smokefree. Indeed some commercial buildings state that the building is smokefree. Would you be willing to stop smoking?

2. Would you be prepared to learn the procedures for civil emergencies? Most organisations need several employees to be responsible for the safe evacuation of a building in the case of earthquakes or other emergencies.

3. Would you regulate your work routine to include exercises to prevent OSS?

# 6

# Paying Tax

The following summary of the New Zealand tax system takes into account all relevant amending legislation effective at 31 March 1994. The tax year is from 1 April to 31 March. A number of legislative changes to tax law came into force on 1 April 1995. The principal legislation is the Income Tax Act 1976.

## PAYING PERSONAL TAX

Income tax is levied under the Income Tax Act 1976 and is charged on most forms of income including business profits, employment income, royalties, interest, dividends and pensions.

The current rates of tax are:

| | |
|---|---|
| Income up to $38,000 | 19.5c for every dollar |
| Income over $38,000 | 33c for every dollar |

## PAY AS YOU EARN

A pay as you earn (PAYE) system of collecting income tax is used for individuals. Income for PAYE purposes falls into two general categories – salaries/wages and other remuneration. PAYE is deducted from these at the time of payment.

At the beginning of each tax year, employees complete a tax code declaration form (IR 21). This becomes a tax deduction certificate when it is returned to the employee at the end of the financial year of when the employee leaves the job. The certificate will show the total amount of income the employee has earned, the tax deducted, any extra pay, tax-free allowances and the period of employment. The employee uses this information to complete a tax return at the end of the tax year (31 March).

Most salary and wage earners file at IR 5 tax return each year. The due date for the completed return to reach Inland Revenue is 7 June each year. You may think that because you are paying tax as you earn, you will not need to pay any extra at the end of the tax year. However, in most cases you will find that you do, unless you are in a situation where you can make deductions for allowable expenses, in which case you may be in the happy situation of being able to claim money back from the Inland Revenue.

## PAYING PROVISIONAL TAX

With business, farming and professional incomes, tax is not deducted at time of receipt but the taxpayer pays 'provisional tax'. A provisional taxpayer is any taxpayer who is liable for paying residual income tax of more than $2,500. 'Residual income tax' is basically the amount of the tax assessed (including any New Zealand Superannuation surcharge), reduced by any tax deductions made from source deduction payment, tax paid overseas, tax paid by trustees, etc. Provisional tax is payable in three instalments. For taxpayers whose balance date is 31 March, payments are made in July, November and March each year. This means that you have to judge how much income you are going to make before you make it! If you underestimate you can be penalised.

Provisional taxpayers use the return form IR 3, which must reach the Inland Revenue Department by 7 July for the majority of taxpayers. Expenses are deducted from the gross business, farming or professional income and tax is calculated on the net income. Credit is given for the provisional tax already paid and for any rebates. If there is an overpayment the taxpayer will receive a refund or credit against future tax. In some situations interest is charged or paid on the under or overpayment of provisional tax.

### Deductible expenses

For people in business, expenses which are incurred in producing income and are relevant and incidental to deriving that income may be claimed as a deduction from income. Expenses of a private, domestic or capital nature are not deductible.

### Claiming exemptions

Income is exempt from tax in New Zealand only if provision is made in the Income Tax Act. Some of the more common items exempt from tax are: maintenance or alimony payments; some war pensions and service disability pensions; income derived from charitable and certain non-profit organisations and also lottery and raffle prizes. Rebates are deducted from the total tax payable.

## Paying tax on your overseas income

New Zealand residents are liable for New Zealand tax on all income including income from overseas. Credit is allowed for any tax paid overseas, but this is limited to the New Zealand tax payable on that income.

## Tax for non-residents

Non-residents are taxed in New Zealand only on income with a New Zealand source. If the income is interest, dividends or royalties, the person is liable for non-resident withholding tax (NRWT), unless the approved issuer levy is paid. NRWT is deducted by the bank or other paying institution.

## Checking your residence status

For tax purposes, individuals are considered to be resident in New Zealand when they fulfil one or more of the following criteria:

● Individuals who have been in New Zealand for more than 183 days in any 12-month period.

● Individuals who have an enduring relationship with New Zealand. This means having strong financial, personal or other such ties with New Zealand. Each case is considered on its own facts.

● Individuals who are away from New Zealand in the service of the New Zealand government.

An individual ceases to be resident in New Zealand if they are:

● Absent from New Zealand for more than 325 days (about 11 months) in any 12-month period and during that time they do not have an enduring relationship with New Zealand.

## PAYING GOODS AND SERVICES TAX

Goods and services tax (GST) is charged at 12.5 per cent on supplies provided in New Zealand by a registered person in the course of a taxable activity.

Anyone with an annual turnover of $30,000 or more must register for GST. Persons registered must charge and collect GST from their customers. GST-registered suppliers of goods and services pay GST on purchases and expenses made in the course of their business but may claim it back later. Registered persons must account for and pay all GST they have collected to the Inland Revenue Department.

GST is charged on the supply of goods and services. Some activities such as salaries and wages, hobby activities, and private sales of personal and domestic items are not taxable. GST is not charged on exempt supplies. Exempt supplies include all financial services, renting of residential property and the sale of donated goods and services by a non-profit organisation.

## PAYING COMPANY TAX

Company taxation is also levied under the Income Tax Act, although companies in New Zealand are taxed in a different way from individual taxpayers. The main differences are that:

- A company does not get any of the special exemptions or rebates that individuals are entitled to:
- Certain dividends paid by a company are exempt in the hands of recipient companies.
- The rate of tax is different.

### Resident companies

A company resident in New Zealand is assessable on all income, whether derived in New Zealand or elsewhere. A company is a New Zealand resident if any of the following criteria apply:

1. It is incorporated in New Zealand.
2. It has its head office in New Zealand.
3. It has its centre of management in New Zealand.
4. Control of the company by its directors is exercised in New Zealand.

Resident companies pay tax on their income at the flat rate of 33 cents in the dollar.

### Special cases

There are various types of companies that have specific methods of assessment. They are: overseas shipping companies, life insurance companies, mining companies and overseas contractors.

### Non-resident companies

A company non-resident in New Zealand is only liable for tax on income derived from New Zealand. Non-resident companies are taxed at 38 cents in the dollar.

Dividends, interest and royalties paid to a non-resident company are subject to withholding tax at a rate specified in the double taxation agreement with the country within which the company is resident. Generally this is the final liability.

## PAYING TAX ON FRINGE BENEFITS

This is a tax at 49 per cent of the value of fringe benefits provided by an employer to an employee. It is payable by the employer on an annual or quarterly basis. Taxable fringe benefits include:

- The private use of a business motor vehicle by an employee.

- Low-interest loans.

- Free, subsidised or discounted transport and other goods and services.

- Employers' contributions to certain employees' superannuation funds and accident, sickness or death benefit funds and insurance policies.

The total fringe benefit tax collected up to 30 June 1998 was $331–393 million.

Can I hear you saying that they would tax the milk in a baby's bottle if they could get it out without the baby screaming!

## AVOIDING DOUBLE TAXATION

Agreements to avoid double taxation have been entered into between New Zealand and Australia, Belgium, Canada, China, Denmark, Fiji, Finland, France, Germany, India, Indonesia, Ireland, Italy, Japan, Korea, Malaysia, Netherlands, Norway, Philippines, Singapore, Sweden, Switzerland, the United Kingdom and the United States. A visitor from one of these countries who receives income for personal services in New Zealand from an overseas employer should refer to the relevant agreement.

## BRINGING CAPITAL WITH YOU

Capital brought into New Zealand is free from tax, and there is no limit on the amount which may be brought into the country. However, income earned from investing that capital is taxable.

## SETTING UP YOUR PENSION

Pensions paid to New Zealand residents by countries with which New Zealand has a double tax agreement are generally exempt from tax in the country of origin and subject to tax in New Zealand. If a pension is taxed in the country of origin, credit is allowed in a New Zealand income tax assessment for the overseas tax paid, up to the amount of New Zealand tax payable on that income.

## GETTING FAMILY SUPPORT

Family Support is provided to people with dependent children who meet income eligibility requirements. It ranges from approximately $47 a week for the first child, to approximately $60 a week per child for a second or subsequent child. Weekly Income New Zealand (WINZ) acts as agent for Inland Revenue in delivering Family Support to beneficiaries; income earners receive it through taxation. For further information contact – website: *http://www.ird.govt.nz*

## CASE STUDIES

### Harry invests

Harry came to New Zealand with $250,000 capital. After he had settled and found himself a job he decided that he would invest his 'spare' capital as he had no immediate use for it. He found an organisation willing to give him 8.5 per cent for a period of six months. This pleased Harry because he decided he would let the interest compound and continue with another six months at the end of his first investment. When he filled in his tax form in April he ignored the part where it asked you to declare interest made on capital, as he has been told that he was able to bring his capital into New Zealand interest free. What Harry failed to notice were the words 'income earned from *investing* that capital is taxable in New Zealand'.

## Marjorie didn't budget

Marjorie had been working for a year in an office in Wellington. She was paid fortnightly and her tax was taken out on a fortnightly basis. At the beginning of April she was sent an IR 5 tax form to complete. She thought that there had been a mistake because she had already paid her tax on a PAYE basis. Upon enquiring at the Inland Revenue Department she was astonished to learn that her PAYE tax was only an estimate and when she duly completed her IR 5 she found that the owed the department a further $400.

## Peter has to pay

Peter was a semi-retired cabinet-maker. He decided to start up a small business doing odd jobs and making small pieces of furniture which he sold when he was ready. His business really picked up and after two years it eventually overtook his part-time job. Peter was pleased that he could finally say he was self-employed, but what he failed to realise was that as he earned over $30,000 per annum with his odd job business he should have registered for GST payments. 12.5 per cent of his total earnings was quite a lot of money for Peter to find in order to clear his tax debt, especially as he had spent most of the money he earned in buying better tools.

## POINTS FOR DISCUSSION

1. If as a self-employed person you didn't accurately assess the provisional tax for the following year's earnings, you could top up the payment when the tax became payable but you might also have to pay an interest charge on the underpayment. Would you think that was fair?

2. If you are paying PAYE on your weekly, fortnightly or monthly earnings you will still have to complete a PAYE form at the end of the tax year, and it is very possible that you may owe more tax as the payments you make on a weekly, fortnightly or monthly basis are only an assessment. Would you be prepared to budget for that eventuality?

3. If your earnings as a self-employed person exceeded $30,000 by only $250 would you be prepared to register for GST?

# 7

## Settling In

### FINDING ACCOMMODATION

Rented accommodation is relatively easy to find in most of the main cities. A modest two or three bedroom home with car parking would cost in the region of $180–$250 per week and higher, depending upon the level of luxury and situation you are seeking. In the better class areas, i.e. Khandallah, Kelburn and Oriental Bay in Wellington, Remuera, St Heliers, Mission Bay and Devonport in Auckland, Cashmere and Opawa in Christchurch, Highcliff and Andersons Bay in Dunedin, it will be more expensive to rent – you could be required to pay anything around $500 and upwards for a desirable property.

If you are a newcomer to New Zealand, the best advice is to rent a property for a while, to enable you to look at the different areas and their proximity to your place of business and choose the property of your liking at leisure. Check the advertisements in the local newspapers, or contact a Real Estate Agency in the locality you have chosen and get a list of the properties they have for rent and sale.

### KNOWING THE SCHOOLING SYSTEM

Early childhood education is available to children under six years old through a wide range of services, most of which are administered by voluntary agencies with government assistance. The Education Act 1989 provides for free education in state primary schools between the ages of five and 19, and attendance is compulsory until the age of 16 years.

Primary school education is compulsory from six years of age, but children usually start formal schooling at the age of five. The final two years of the primary course, forms 1 and 2, may be taken at a full primary school, an intermediate school, an area school, or a form 1–7 school depending on where a child lives. On completing

JOHNSONVILLE. 2br fully renovated cottage with garden, garage and new kitchen. $200pw.

J'VILLE exec, sunny, quiet, 5-6 br home. Views, bush, garden, carport, d/washer, w/mach, near mall $325neg.

KARORI. 2 bedroom, unfurn flat, exc cond. private. $185pw.

KARORI (city end) 3 dbr house, whiteware, sunny, close bus, no dogs. $250pw.

KARORI, city end, 2br flat, open plan, unfurn, redec, carpark, $200.

KELBURN: 2br flat, good cond, close to bus & Varsity. $150pw.

KILBIRNIE 2 brm, harbour views, exc cod. $180pw.

KHANDALLAH, 1 br sunny partially furn flat, drive-on, BBQ area, $170pw.

LOWER HUTT/Kelson, 3 br 8yr old house, long-term only, $195pw.

KARORI, quality 3 dbr house, 4 car gge, $925pw.

KARORI, exc mod 3br t/ house, w/ware, existing embassy rep returning. Avail end of Sept. $400pw.

THORNDON, newly restored 3 bedroom house, fully furn & equipped to the last detail. Parking. Close to city, gardens, shops. $550pw.

THORNDON, brand new 2br + garage. Close to city. $275pw.

TITAHI BAY, Onepoto. 3 br unfurn hse, good access, garage, view, $200pw.

TITAHI BAY mod 3br hse, views, no pets, $195pw.

TWO br unfurn flat, sunny, views, tidy. Wilton, $160pw.

UPPER HUTT, Fergusson Dr. 2 br flat, sunny, gas heating, washing machine. $140pw.

UPPER HUTT, Central, tidy. 2 br flat, handy schools & shops, $115pw.

UPPER HUTT. 2 br flat, washing machine, carport, lockup shed. $120pw.

UPPER HUTT: Sunny 2 br flat, furn, carpeted, curtains, garage. $140pw.

VOGELTOWN, 3 br farmhouse kitchen, large lounge, all day sun, fully furn, from Oct 1-Feb 6. $280pw. References reqd.

KHANDALLAH $259,000: Colonial charmer. Relax and enjoy this immacuately presented home with 3 dble brms, study, going with internal entry on a 753m² garden section in a very handy location.

KHANDALLAH $135,000: Karachi chop! Yes 3 bedroom home with the price chopped to $135,000. Central Khadallah. Needs a lover – invest and win.

KHANDALLAH $169,000 Character Plus. Fabulous 2 dble brm character home that receive wonderful sun. Drive on – great location. Be quick.

KHANDALLAH $370,000: Choose your decor. New low maintenance architect desinged 4 brm (ens) home with dual living areas and double garaging nearing completion on golfers section close to village.

KHANDALLAH $255,000: Vacation at home by your heated and covered pool. Superb harbour views. 4 brms, rumpus, new kitchen, dble garage.

CHURTON PARK $146,000: Substantial sun soaked, spacious 3 brm family home, garage. Enjoy the brilliant sunsets and country views.

CHURTON PARK $238,000: Completely refurnished and no expense spared! New kitchen/family room.

CROFTON DOWNS GV $160,000. A real charmer. Appealing 3 brm single level home with garaging beneath. Pleasant outlook and well sited for shops and public transport. Offers invited.

GRENADA VILLAGE $149,000: Features huge living space and a huge tradesman's gara/workshop. Sun filled conservatory, 3 brms, lovely garden and views.

HATAITAI $190,000: Enjoy living close to the village in this 3 brm character home with lots of sun, garaging and off street parking.

WHITBY, 2 br townhouse, $250pw.

Fig. 4. A selection of property advertisements.

form 2, usually after eight years' school attendance, a child normally enters form 3 of a secondary school, or alternatively form 3 in an area or form 1–7 school.

Primary and secondary schools are required to be open for at least 394 half days and 380 half days, respectively, each year. The school year is divided into three terms. The first term commences usually on the fifth Monday of the year (in secondary schools, the fifth Monday or Tuesday). Boards of trustees may apply to vary their schools' terms and holidays to take local circumstances into account. In 1995, some schools will follow a four-term year and a few will follow a six-term year.

## BECOMING A KIWI

### Pubs
The New Zealand way of life is quite different from the British. Until recently there were no cosy pubs where you could wind down at the end of the day, or enjoy an entertaining evening out. A few smaller pubs have now started to appear but on the whole the pubs are large and noisy, with strange elbow-high tables scattered around the rooms where the men seem to enjoy standing and leaning while drinking their beer. Until roughly 25 years ago, drinking was referred to as 'the six o'clock swill'. That was because pubs closed at 6.00 p.m., and everyone had to drink their drink quickly and leave.

### Restaurants
A new trend that seems to becoming extremely popular is 'dining out'. In Wellington alone there are enough restaurants for you to dine out at a different one every day of the year! Wine bars are also very popular with the younger set, and in some you may find live music.

### Cinema
It would seem, according to recent figures in the local press, that New Zealanders are the world's most avid cinema-goers. Cinema complexes which hold two, three or even four screens are springing up all over the main cities.

### 'Bring a plate'
It is very common to be invited to an evening gathering of friends and be asked to 'bring a plate'. This doesn't mean an empty plate!

You are expected to concoct some delicacy and share it with everyone else who will be doing the same thing. When I first came to New Zealand I innocently took along an empty plate, thinking perhaps that the hostess was running short of crockery – I remember the strange looks I got!

## Dress

Dress here is rather casual, so aim for the middle of the road look if you are unsure as to how you should dress for an event that doesn't indicate the requirements. Shirts and trousers for the men, both can be short in the summer. Until you are sure of the expectations, the ladies should dress simply, not over dressy. Don't wear the crown jewels until you have found your ground.

## PLAYING THE GAME

Sport is the life, blood and soul of a great majority of New Zealanders, the national game being rugby. Weekends during the season are taken up with games being played all over the country, and television is completely taken over at weekends with replays, and then replays of the replays!

Parents of young children can be seen huddled against the cold supporting their young prodigy's efforts on the field. Very young kiwis can even be seen doing the 'haka' before their interclub matches begin. They all have aspirations to be another Jonah Lomu. Netball is very popular for girls, as is hockey. In the summer tennis clubs are popping at the seams with likely players, and there will invariably be a waiting list to join.

New Zealand is generously endowed with wonderful golf courses. The green fees vary, but at weekends you can expect to pay around $20 for 18 holes.

Water sports are high on the activity list with sailing being very popular. After winning the America's Cup in 1995, the continual talk has been of yachting. The harbours and lakes can be seen to be cluttered with a myriad of sailing boats. In fact most families enjoy time on the water during the summer, whether being propelled by wind or motor.

## CASE STUDIES

### Russell and Jenny compromise

Russell and Jenny secured employment in Wellington. Jenny wanted to buy a house straight away, and feel settled. However, Russell couldn't decide which area of the suburbs he would like to live in. After two very tiring weeks of house searching, they decided that it would be very sensible if they rented a house for six months, which would enable them to look around at leisure, and also get to know the areas. Exactly six months after they moved to New Zealand, they bought a house in Johnsonville, because of the convenience of the train which took them right into Wellington, and the fact that there was an abundance of shops, which meant they didn't need to travel far to find a good selection of supermarkets.

### The Grays make a decision

When Alison and David came to New Zealand their son James was four years old. Alison wanted to work to help out with the finances so they rented a house quite close to town which meant that David didn't have long trips to work every day. Alison found a kindergarten for James, and she got part-time work in a supermarket. James didn't settle at kindergarten, he was quiet and withdrawn. The kindergarten teacher spoke to Alison when she came to pick James up at home time. She told her that she thought there had been too many changes for James. Leaving England and then being parted from his parents had made him feel insecure. Alison and David made the decision to keep James at home, and Alison had to relinquish her job. This meant that their income dropped, but they both agreed that their son's well-being was of paramount importance, and that they could increase their income and build up their savings when he was five years old and able to go to school – by then he would have found his feet in his adopted country.

### Catherine finds out

Catherine was desperately seeking a change from her office job in Manchester. All her friends had married, and somehow she had been left behind. She wanted some excitement in her life, so she decided that she would go to New Zealand. Finding a job was easy as she was very well qualified in the computer field. After two years she realised that she didn't like the laid-back style of life in new Zealand. She made the decision and booked her flight back to

England. She didn't go back to Manchester upon her return, she moved to Oxford where she slotted back into the English lifestyle without blinking an eye.

## POINTS FOR DISCUSSION

1. Are you prepared for the inevitable home sickness that most people experience?

2. Would you be prepared to rent a home while you explored the possibilities of life in New Zealand?

3. The main sporting focus in New Zealand is rugby, to the exclusion of many other sports. Would this aggravate you?

# 8

## Careers and Professions

### IS THIS YOU?

Accountant

Advertising Manager

Agricultural Manager

Barrister

Builder

Caterer

Clerical Worker

Computer Operator

Doctor

Economist

Farmer

Financial Manager

Lecturer

Nurse

Pharmacist

Physiotherapist

Professor

Real Estate Agent

Teacher

Veterinarian

WP Operator

Psychologist

Tutor

Receptionist

Electronic Engineer

Medical Secretary

Aviation Worker

Beautician

Chiropractor

Dentist

Engineer

Lawyer

Optometrist

Podiatrist

Surveyor

Secretary

Solicitor

Telecommunications Expert

Dental Technician

## GETTING STARTED

Finding the right job may not be easy, so the better prepared you are the more chances you have of finding one. Here are a few ideas to get you started.

Make sure you have an up-to-date Curriculum Vitae (CV) prepared. Curriculum Vitae is Latin for 'Course of Life'. It should contain two or three pages of information. A CV is your personal sales document. It details all the skills and experiences that you've gained, your interests and hobbies and your work history. Most employers ask for a CV or Résumé. Its main purpose is to get you an interview. Résumé is French for 'Summary'. A résumé is usually one page of information about yourself, but not in as much detail as a CV. If an employer asks for a résumé instead of a CV this usually means they would like just the information most relevant to the job.

The main types of CVs are:

● functional

● chronological.

### Creating a functional CV

This highlights the particular skills you have that match a specific job you are applying for. A functional CV will have:

● a clearly stated job objective (relevant to the job you are applying for)

● your skills directly related to the job objective

● a brief list of your work history, and

● details of your education and training.

If you are applying for different jobs, prepare a different CV for each job application. Each CV should highlight the skills you have that best fit the job you are applying for. (See Figure 5.)

### Creating a chronological CV

This is a record of all your jobs and education in the order you did them. A chronological CV is a very structured CV and can be used for a variety of job applications. (See Figure 6.)

| Personal Details | |
| --- | --- |
| Name | Aroha Hylton |
| Address | 1/80 Pine Crescent |
| | Blockhouse Bay |
| | Auckland |
| Telephone | 0-9-882-0956 |

**Objective**  To further develop my supervisory skills

**Highlights of experience**
- Three years' experience as assistant Check-Out Supervisor
- Trained new staff in supermarket procedures

**Relevant Experience**

*Numeracy Skills*
Dealing with numbers/figures has always been my specialty. My background includes:
- treasurer for local sports club and association (hockey)
- balancing my own and friend's cheque books
- helping friends budget their finances

*Organisation skills*
I pay attention to detail and can delegate effectively. My organisation skills have developed well and this is shown in my involvement with:
- social functions for work
- fundraising for local sports club
- written correspondence for cricket club

*Communication skills*
My communication skills are excellent. I pride myself in being able to put my view across in an assertive manner. I have:
- captained a local hockey team – guiding and directing team members
- experience as assistant check-out supervisor for three years
- attended courses on effective communication skills

**Employment History**
1989–1993 General Food Supermarket – Assistant Check-out Supervisor
1987–1988 Foodtown Supermarket – Shop Assistant

**Education/Training**
1986–1987 Regional Polytechnic
          Effective Communication Skills
1982–1985 Four years secondary education

**Referees**

**Ms Kay Arland** (Check-out Supervisor)
General Food Supermarket, Henderson
Telephone: 0-9-345 9876

**Mr W Whetu** (Sports Co-ordinator)
Sports Foundation
Telephone: 0-9-234 8765

Fig. 5. Sample functional CV.

**Personal Details**
Name              Matthew Reid
Address          57 Kowhai Street
                  Brighton
                  Christchurch
Telephone       0-3-234 5678

**Personal Statement**       Throughout my school and working career I have prided myself on being a self motivated, reliable and hardworking person. More than anything, these are the qualities I wish to recommend to you.

**Education and Training**
     1993        **Carrington Polytechnic**
                  Training Opportunity Programme (TOPs course)
                  Building and Landscaping Skills
     1984–1987 **Mt Albert Grammar School**
                  Subjects taken at sixth form level:
                  Horticulture and Art

**Work History**
     1988-1993 **Harvey's Brick & Blocklayers**
                  Labourer
                  Duties included: heavy lifting, spreading sand and gravel, laying bricks into patterns and driving.
                  Position made redundant when the firm was sold.
     1987–1988 **Robinson & Walker Construction**
                  Builder's Labourer (temporary)
                  Duties included: Cleaning tools, measuring to instructions, assisting tradesmen with general duties.
     1987        **Beechcroft's Orchards – Henderson**
                  Vineyard Labourer (seasonal)
                  Duties included: General duties, packing, cleaning sheds

**Additional information**      Clean driver's licence (A, B, F)
                  Own reliable transport

**Interests/Hobbies**      Running, squash, landscape gardening

**Referees**      **Keith Harvey** (former manager Harvey's Brick & Blocklayers
                  37 Oakland Avenue
                  Glen Eden
                  Auckland
                  Telephone: 0-9-345 6789

                  **Susan Anderson** (owner of Beachcroft's Orchards)
                  88 Rimu Drive
                  Henderson
                  Auckland
                  Telephone: 0-9-876 5432

Fig. 6. Sample chronological CV.

## What about references?

References, either written or verbal, are very important. They tell an employer what you are like as a worker or how well you have worked.

You need to ask the person whose name you want to use as a verbal reference on your CV if it's alright with them.

If you don't have written references, you could ask for one from someone you have done some voluntary work for. You could also ask for a reference from someone, other than family, who has known you a while.

## FINDING JOB LEADS

Did you know that 70 per cent of jobs are not advertised? These are usually the jobs that are found by people who do their own job seeking. There is more to finding a job than just looking in the local newspaper. The following are vital sources of job openings:

- professional publications
- professional associations
- the Head Office of the organisation you would like to work in
- advertising in the paper yourself for the job you are seeking
- circulating your details to professional organisations and consultants.

## TACKLING TYPICAL INTERVIEW QUESTIONS

The following are some typical questions used by employers when interviewing for job vacancies. What would your answers be?

- Why do you want to work here?
- What interests you most about this job?
- Have you done this type of work before?
- Why should we hire you and not someone else?
- What skills can you bring to this job?
- Tell me about yourself, your hobbies and other interests?

- What are your strengths and weaknesses?
- How well do you work with other people?
- What did you most enjoy about your last job?
- Why did you leave your last job?
- What are your plans for the future?
- What level of wage or salary do you want?
- Who can we contact for a reference?

The following are some questions you might like to ask at an interview:

- Could you tell me more about the job?
- Where and with whom would I be working?
- What are the dress standards?
- Are there other conditions or requirements?
- When will you decide who gets the job?

## CHOOSING YOUR OCCUPATION

Below are described some of the opportunities available in a wide range of careers and professions. Useful addresses are listed to help you follow up particular areas of interest and obtain more detailed information. At the end of the chapter there is a comprehensive list of personnel consultants who may also be able to advise and assist you.

### Advertising

I was told by Saatchi & Saatchi Advertising in Wellington that they are always on the look out for new exceptional talent. There are several people from England and Australia already working in their office. The best advice I can give is for you to contact any of the advertising agencies listed below, and they will be able to give you up-to-date information on their needs.

*Useful addresses*
Saatchi & Saatchi Advertising, PO Box 6540, Wellington. Tel: 64-4-385 6524; Fax: 64-4-385 9678.

Colenso Communications Ltd, 138 The Terrace, Wellington. Tel: 64-4-473 7177.

Donnithorne Fordyce Vintiner Birss & Young, 128–132 The Terrace, Wellington. Tel: 64-4-473 1129.

HKM Advertising Ltd, PO Box 2211, Wellington. Tel: 64-4-385 2069; Fax: 64-4-385 1645.

McCann Erickson Ltd, 8 Lipman Street, Mt Victoria, Wellington. Tel: 64-4-385 0248; Fax: 64-4-385 2113.

## Aviation

The aviation industry in New Zealand comprises the commercial airlines, e.g. Air New Zealand and Ansett. There are numerous small airlines, e.g. Air Chathams which operates from the Chatham Islands; Gt Barrier Airlines which operates from Gr Barrier Island; Mr Cook Airlines; Rex Aviation, specialist in corporate jets, turbo props, freight operations and aircraft charters; Soundsair, which operates an amphibian service to the Marlborough Sounds and three scheduled flights daily from Wellington to Picton plus charter flights anywhere in New Zealand.

There are aviation opportunities available in New Zealand and it would be a good start to contact the following:

*Useful addresses:*
The Civil Aviation Authority of New Zealand, PO Box 31-441, Lower Hutt, Wellington. Tel: 64-4-560 9400; Fax: 64-4-569 2024. Website: *http://www.caa.govt.nz*

Aviation Industry Association, Agriculture House, 12 Johnstone Street, Wellington. Tel: 64-4-472 2707. Website: *http:// www.caa.govt.nz*

Massey School of Aviation, Private Bag 11222, Palmerston North. Tel: 64-6-356 9099. (Training and general aviation enquiries.) Website: *http://www.massey.ac.nz*

## Accountancy

McLay & So (NZ) Ltd of Wellington recently informed me that the market is fairly buoyant for accountants with banking backgrounds and manufacturing backgrounds.

Firstly check out if your qualifications enable you do work in New Zealand by contacting the New Zealand Society of Accountants, PO Box 11-342, Wellington. Tel: 64-4-473 8544; Fax: 64-4-472 6282.

*Useful addresses*
Chartered Institute of Management Accountants, PO Box 11269, Wellington. Tel: 64-4-384 7393; Fax: 64-4-385 4279.

## Agriculture

Even though there is unemployment in New Zealand there is still a demand for *skilled* agricultural labour. The government has allowed Marvin Farm Services to bring a limited number of overseas young farmers into New Zealand to participate in their Agricultural Work Study Tour. Well over 500 young farmers have undertaken this programme in the last ten years. The requirements to apply for entry to this scheme are for young farmers to have sound practical dairy farming experience.

The North Island of New Zealand is mainly rolling contour with dairy farming on the lowlands and sheep and cattle on the hills. The South Island is very mountainous, with mainly sheep, arable and beef farming.

The summer season commences in November and ends about the middle of March. Winter conditions vary between mild and wet in the North Island and cold and snowy in the South Island.

As New Zealand is an agricultural country, most of its earnings come from producing and exporting butter, milk products, meat and wool. Marvin Farm Services provide a service to farmers, supplying them with labour when they are short-handed because of sickness, holidays or extra work.

Barry Hazlehurst of Marvin Farm Services advises me that successful applicants *must* arrive between mid July and early August. This is when dairy farmers require staff to assist them over the calving period. Overseas young farmers can almost be assured of a full work programme from this time until mid February or possibly a full 12 months. At times Marvin Farm Services send labour to Western Australia during the wheat-planting season in April through to the end of June.

Some important points to remember:

● Marvin Farm Services only employ young farmers from the United Kingdom and Ireland.

- They arrange temporary work permits for *successful* applicants.
- The scheme starts in July or very early August each year.
- *Compulsory* seven months work although up to 12 months work available.
- Successful applicants must have had a fair amount of practical dairy farming experience.
- Preferred age is 20–30 and you *must* be single.

For further details about this Work Study Tour please contact: Barry Hazlehurst, Marvin Farm Services, PO Box 248, Matamata. Tel: 64-7-888 6025; Fax: 64-7-888 5014.

Lance Orr of Central Employment informs me that he employs backpackers for farm work during the July/August period. If you travel to New Zealand as a visitor on a visitor's permit you are *not* allowed to work until you have applied for and received a work permit from the Immigration Department. For further information please contact: Lance Orr, Central Employment, R.D.1, Tuakau, South Auckland. Tel: 64-9-233 4885; Fax: 64-9-233 4889. Email: *Lance@ps.gen.nz*

*Useful addresses*
Ministry of Agriculture and Forestry, Wellington. Website: *http://www.maf.gov.nz*

Halford R. E. & Associates Ltd, Kist Building, Mahara Place, Whakatane, Bay of Plenty. Tel: 64-7-293 2437.

Federated Farmers of New Zealand Inc, Box 715, Wellington. Tel: 64-4-473 7269; Fax: 64-4-473 1081. Website: *http://www.fedfarm.org.nz* Email: *Wellingtonoffice@fedfarm.org.nz*

New Zealand Dairy Board, Box 417, Wellington. Tel: 64-4-471 8300; Fax: 64-4-471 8600. Website: *http://www.nzdb.com* or *http://www.nzmilk.com*

Meat New Zealand, PO Box 121, Wellington. Tel: 64-4-473 9150; Fax: 64-4-472 3172. Website: *http://www.meatnz.co.nz*

New Zealand Wool Board, Box 3225, Wellington. Tel: 67-4-472 6888; Fax: 64-4-473 7872. Website: *http://www.nzwool.co.nz*

## Automotive mechanical engineers

The Motor Trade Association Inc indicated that there is a shortage of automotive mechanical engineers in New Zealand because of a shortage of apprentices. If you:

- have City & Guilds qualifications
- are versatile with all makes and models
- are willing to live anywhere in New Zealand
- have your own tools

then you can start tomorrow!

To find vacancies you should arrange to receive copies of New Zealand newspapers:

*The New Zealand Herald*, Box 32, Auckland (whole of NZ). Website: *http://www.netclassifieds.co.nz*

*The Dominion*, Box 3740, Wellington (North Island).

*The Otago Daily Times*, Box 517, Dunedin (South Island).

*The Christchurch Star*, Box 1467, Christchurch (South Island).

Write to the paper of your choice enclosing N$8 per copy. You can pay by cheque, credit card or bank draft.

*Useful addresses*

Motor Trade Association Inc, Box 9244, Courtenay Place, Wellington. Tel: 64-4-385 8859; Fax: 64-4-385 9517. Website: *http://www.mta.org.nz* Email: *mta@motor-trade.co.nz*

Institute of Automotive Mechanical Engineers, 89 Courtenay Place, Wellington. Tel: 64-4-293 1900; Fax: 64-4-293 1934.

## Building trades

Qualification requirements are the same as in the UK. There are limited job opportunities available. Vacancies are usually advertised in the newspapers. Direct all enquiries to the Building Industry Authority.

*Useful address*

Building Industry Authority, PO Box 11846, Wellington. Tel: 64-4-471 0794; Fax: 64-4-471 0798. Website: *http://www.bia.co.nz*

Email: *bia@bia.co.nz*

The New Zealand telephone directory is now on the web. Website: *http://www.whitepages.co.nz* and *http://www.yellowpages.co.nz*

**Beauty therapy**
More and more women are taking advantage of the wide range of services, such as aromatherapy, waxing, manicure, pedicure, acne treatment, therapeutic massage, electrolysis, facials, red vein treatment, etc., now available from beauty therapy clinics. Jobs in this area can be found in the newspapers. For further information contact Association of Beauty Therapists, Box 28026, Remuera, Auckland 5. Tel: 64-9-303 3238.

**Hairdressing**
It would be advisable to look in the newspaper in the area of your choice for hairdressing positions. (For details of newspapers, see above under Automotive mechanical engineers.)

**Catering and hospitality industry**
There is real growth in the restaurant industry, with Wellington alone having more restaurants than days in the year. Jobs in this area can usually be found in the newspapers. The hotel industry is expanding to accommodate the large influx of visitors to New Zealand. Two of the larger hotel chains are:

Quality Hotels, Box 5640 Wellesley Street, Auckland. Tel: 64-9-309 4411; Fax: 64-9-377 0764. Website: *http://www.cdlhotels.co.nz*

Southern Pacific Hotel Corporation, Box 3921, Auckland. Tel: 64-9-373 2269; Fax: 64-9-309 3577. Website: *http://www.sphc.com.au*

*Some ski resort hotels*
Southern Cross Ski Hotel, Canterbury. Tel: 64-3-302 8464.
Mount Hutt Country Club, Canterbury. Tel: 64-3-302 8721.
Edgewater Resort, Wanaka, Central Otago. Tel: 64-3-443 8311.
Quality Hotel Terraces, Queenstown. Tel: 64-3-442 7950.
The Queenstown Parkroyal, Queenstown. Tel: 64-3-442 7750.
Gold Ridge Hotel, 334 Frankton Road, Queenstown. Tel: 64-3-442 6500. Fax: 64-3-442 7898. Website: *http://www.nz.com/travel/ scenicCircle/*
A-Line Hotel, 27 Stanley Street, Queenstown. Tel: 64-3-442 7700;

Fax: 64-3-442 7755. Website: *http://www.nz.com/travel/scenic Circle/*

## Chiropractors

Chiropractic clinics can be found in most centres. They are widely used for sporting injuries and general consultation. For further details contact the New Zealand Chiropractic Association.

*Useful address*
New Zealand Chiropractic Association, Box 7144, Wellesley Street, Auckland. Tel: 64-9-373 4343; Fax: 64-9-373 5973.

## Computing

John Jennings of IDPE Holdings Limited, Wellington, informed me that the skills which are especially short in New Zealand at the moment include relational database, open systems, client server and networking. Although relatively newer skills such as Oracle, C++, Windows, object-oriented programming, business process re-engineering and SAP are in demand, there has been a resurgence of interest in mainframe skills such as Cobol/CICS and DB2. Good mid-range experience is also sought on a regular basis.

A Ministry of Commerce survey revealed an increase of more than 10 per cent in the number of people employed in the IT industry since 1989. The report also revealed that salaries for people with highly specialised skills increased by 15–20 per cent.

Employers looking for contract staff focus primarily on the technical skills of an applicant, but for permanent roles a real commitment to remain in New Zealand is as important as anything else. Britain is a logical market from which to recruit staff for New Zealand because of cultural similarities, language and past experience.

## Dentistry and dental technicians

Private dental practitioners and government agencies collaborate to provide oral health care in New Zealand. The school dental service, staffed by operating auxiliaries, is a distinctive feature of the system.

There were 1,496 dentists in the active workforce in 1998. The New Zealand Dental Association is recognised as the organised voice of dental practitioners and approximately 95 per cent of registered dentists belong. The Dental Association Council is the Association's governing body. More information can be had by using the website. Website: *http://www.dentalcouncil.org.nz*

Clinical dental technicians are able to supply and fit dentures directly to the public. They are represented by the Institute of Dental Technologists. Contact the Dental Technicians Board for more information.

There are many overseas-trained doctors and dentists registered as unemployed. In many cases this is because their qualifications are not sufficient to allow them to practise in New Zealand. They are required to sit an expensive three-part Medical Council registration exam, which I am told many fail at the first attempt.

*Useful address*
Dental Technicians Board, PO Box 11053, Ellerslie, Auckland. Tel: 64-9-579 7096. Fax: 64-9-525 1169. Website: *http://www.nzhis.govt.nz/stats/dental,stats.html*

Dental Council of New Zealand. Website: *http://www.dentalcouncil. org.nz*

**Teachers**
Teachers in New Zealand are mainly hired by the Board of Trustees of the school where they seek employment. The Trustees also negotiate salaries. It is essential to check that your qualifications are acceptable in New Zealand by contacting the Teacher Registration Board, Box 5326, Wellington. Tel: 64-4-471 0852; Fax: 64-4-471 0870. Website: *http://www.trb.govt.nz* For more teaching information contact website: *http:www.teachnz.govt.nz*

Positions are advertised in the newspapers (see above under Automotive mechanical engineers for details) and in *Teachers Gazette*, available from the New Zealand Education Institute, PO Box 466, Wellington. Tel: 64-4-384 9609; Fax: 64-4-385 1772. Email: *nzei@ei.org.nz*

**Lecturers and professors**
There are seven universities in New Zealand. They all offer courses in a wide range of subjects in the arts, social sciences, commerce and science. Law and music courses are available at Auckland, Victoria, Canterbury and Otago. Most universities specialise in certain fields.

Contact can be made with the university of your choice from the following addresses:

*North Island*
University of Auckland, Private Bag 92019, Auckland. Tel: 64-9-373 7513; Fax; 64-9-373 7405. Website: *http://www.auckland.ac.nz*

University of Waikato, Private Bag 3015, Hamilton. Tel: 64-7-856 2889; Fax: 64-7-838 4370. Website: *http://www.waikato.ac.nz*

Massey University, Private Bag 11-222, Palmerston North. Tel: 64-6-356 9099; Fax: 64-6-350 5630. Website: *http://www.massey.ac.nz*

Victoria University of Wellington, Box 600, Wellington. Tel: 64-4-472 1000; Fax: 64-6-499 4601. Website: *http://www.vuw.ac.nz*

*South Island*
Canterbury University, Private Bag 4800, Christchurch. Tel: 64-3-366 7001; Fax: 64-3-364 2999. Website: *http://www.canterbury.ac.nz*

Lincoln University, PO Box 94, Canterbury. Tel: 64-3-325 2811; Fax: 64-3-325 2965. Website: *http://www.lincoln.ac.nz*

Otago University, PO Box 56, Dunedin. Tel: 64-3-479 1100; Fax: 64-3-474 1607. Website: *http://www.otago.ac.nz*

The current salary scales and ranges are:

| Lecturers: | A scale from $42,000 to $52,000 pa |
|---|---|
| Senior Lecturers: | A scale from $55,000 to $63,000 (bar) A scale from $66,000 to $70,000 pa |
| Associate Professors: | A range from $73,000 to $79,000 pa |
| Professors: | A range from $82,000 to $102,000 pa |

### Economists, finance and banking
The most likely sources of employment are through the banks.

*Useful addresses*
ANZ Banking Group (NZ) Ltd, Box 1492, Wellington. Tel: 64-4-496 7000; Fax: 64-4-473 6919.

ASB Bank (Auckland Savings Bank), Hunter Street, Wellington.

Tel: 64-4-499 4422; Fax: 64-4-499 7766.

Bank of New Zealand, 1 Willis Street, Wellington. Tel: 64-4-474 6999; Fax: 64-4-474 6531.

National Bank of NZ Limited, 170-186 Featherston Street, Wellington Tel: 64-4-494 4000; Fax: 64-4-473 6959.

Reserve Bank of New Zealand, 2 The Terrace, Wellington. Tel: 64-4-472 2029; Fax: 64-4-473 8554.

Westpac Banking Corporation, 318-324 Lambton Quay, Wellington. Tel: 64-4-498 1000; Fax: 64-4-498 1701.

**Health**
There are 23 CHEs (hospitals) in New Zealand. Take your choice from the following list, and send off your CV or resumé.

Northland Health, PO Box 742, Whangerei. Tel: 64-9-438 2070; Fax: 64-9-430 8010.

Waitemata Health, Private Bag 93-503, Takapuna, Auckland. Tel: 64-9-486 1491; Fax: 64-9-486 8908.

Auckland Healthcare, Greenlane/National Womens Hospitals, Green Lane West, Epsom, Auckland 1003. Tel: 64-9-638 9909 (Greenlane) and 64-9-638 9919 (National Womens).

South Auckland Health, Middlemore Hospital, Private Bag 93311, Otahuhu, Auckland. Tel: 64-9-276 0053; Fax: 64-9-276 0023.

Health Waikato, PO Box 934, Hamilton. Tel: 64-7-839 8899. Fax: 64-7-839 8879.

Western Bay Health, Tauranga Hospital, Private Bag 12-024, Tauranga, Bay of Plenty. Tel: 64-7-579 8000; Fax: 64-7-579 8487.

Eastbay Health, Whakatane Hospital, PO Box 241, Whakatane. Tel: 64-7-307 8999.

Lakeland Health, Rotorua Hospital, Private Bag 3023, Rotarua. Tel: 64-7-348 1199; Fax: 64-7-378 2033.

Tairawhiti Healthcare Ltd, Gisborne Hospital, Private Bag 7001, Gisborne. Tel: 64-6-868 0001; Fax: 64-6-867 8527.

Taranaki Healthcare, Private Bag 2016, New Plymouth. Tel: 64-6-757 5439; Fax: 64-6-753 6139.

Healthcare Hawkes Bay, Private Bag 6023, Napier. Tel: 64-6-878 1600; Fax: 64-6-835 0666.

Good Health Wanganui, Wanganui Hospital, Private Bag, Wanganui. Tel: 64-6-348 1234; Fax: 64-6-345 9390.

Midcentral Health, PO Box 2056, Palmerston North. Tel: 64-6-350 8061; Fax: 64-6-355 0616.

Capital Coast Health, Private Bag, 7902, Wellington South. Tel: 64-4-385 5900; Fax: 64-4-385 5929.

Hutt Valley Health, Private Bag 31-907, Lower Hutt. Tel: 64-4-566 6999; Fax: 64-4-570 4424.

Wairarapa Health, Masterton Hospital, PO Box 96, Masterton. Tel: 64-6-378 2099; Fax: 64-6-378 2110.

Nelson Marlborough Health, PO Box 132, Nelson. Tel: 64-3-546 1800; Fax: 64-3-546 9326.

Coast Health Care, PO Box 387, Greymouth. Tel: 64-3-768 0499; Fax: 64-3-768 2791.

Canterbury Health, PO Box 1600, Christchurch. Tel: 64-3-364 0460; Fax: 64-3-364 0252.

Healthlink South, PO Box 800, Christchurch. Tel: 64-3-337 7728; Fax: 64-4-337 7717.

Health South Canterbury Ltd, Private Bag 911, Timaru. Tel: 64-3-688 1079; Fax: 64-3-688 0238.

Healthcare Otago, Private Bag 1921, Dunedin. Tel: 64-3-474 0999; Fax: 64-3-474 7639.

Southern Health, PO Box 828, Invercargill. Tel: 64-3-218 1949; Fax: 64-3-218 1949.

Jobs within the health industry are advertised in the daily newspapers. (For details of newspapers, see above under Automotive mechanical engineers.) A health publication is also available – *NZ Health Employment Gazette*. It is published fortnightly. To get a regular copy of this publication you should write to PO Box 68 450, Newton, Auckland. Tel: 64-9-358 2255. Website: *http://www.scpublishing.co.nz* Individual subscriptions are available at $48 per annum.

To give you an idea of its contents, here is a small sample of the vacancies:

- Community Psychiatrist wanted in Hastings
- Consultant Physician wanted in Balclutha
- Dietitian wanted in Hawkes Bay
- Domicilary Physiotherapist wanted in Otago
- Fire Safety Officer wanted in Southland
- Intermediate Practitioner wanted in Whangarei
- Manager – Operating Theatre wanted in Southland
- Manager Sterile Supply Services wanted in Wellington
- Medical Radiation Technologists wanted in Wellington
- Midwives wanted in Wellington
- Nurse wanted in Dunedin
- Speech Language Therapist wanted in Wanganui
- Sonographer (registered MRT, with diploma in Medical Ultrasound) wanted in Wanganui
- Pharmacist – Locum wanted in Dunedin
- Health Analyst wanted in Hamilton.

## Doctors
Firstly and most importantly, you will need to find out if your qualifications will enable you to be registered as a doctor in New Zealand by contacting the Medical Council of New Zealand. Don't

even pack a teaspoon *before* you have done this! The New Zealand Medical Association advises that the employment situation for junior doctors in New Zealand is not very promising at the moment.

*Useful addresses*
Medical Council of New Zealand, 139–143 Willis Street, Wellington. Tel: 64-4-384 7635; Fax: 64-4-385 8902.

Royal NZ College of General Practitioners, 388 The Terrace, Wellington. Tel: 64-4-496 5999; Fax: 64-4-496 5997. Email: *rnzcgp@rnzcgp.org.nz*

Royal Australasian College of Physicians, St John House, 99 The Terrace, Wellington. Tel: 64-4-472 6713; Fax: 64-4-472 6718.

Royal Australasian College of Surgeons, Box 7451, Wellington. Tel: 64-4-385 8247; Fax: 64-4-385 8873. Email: *racs@surgeons.co.nz*

The following locum agencies arrange partnerships and sale of practices:

Auckland Medical Bureau, PO Box 37753 Parnell, Auckland. Tel: 64-9-377 5903. Email: *doctors-amb.nz@extra.co.nz*

*Useful publications*
*The NZ Medical Journal* which is published by the Medical Council.
*The New Zealand Doctor*, Box 33124, Takapuna, Auckland 9.
*The GP Weekly*, Private Bag 65-901, Mairangi Bay, Auckland.

## Nursing
Vacancies can be found in the local newspapers and other publications, as mentioned at the beginning of the health section.

*More useful addresses*
Nursing Council of New Zealand, 97–99 Courtenay Place, Wellington. Tel: 64-4-385 9589; Fax: 64-4-801 8502.

*Private nursing agencies*
Nightingale Nurses Ltd, Box 54 137, Plimmerton, Wellington. Tel: 64-4-239 9230.

Community Domiciliary Nursing Trust, Box 30-814 Lower Hutt, Wellington. Tel: 64-4-567 6097 or 570 0266.

Duty Calls Nursing & Homecare Ltd, Box 10 720, Wellington South. Tel: 64-4-499 1777.

Acorn Healthlink, 72 Dominion Road, Auckland. Tel: 64-9-630 8300; Fax: 64-9-623 9622.

Drake Medox, 99 Atkinson Avenue, Otahu. Tel: 64-9-276 5342; Fax: 64-9-276 8903. Website: http://www.drakeintl.com

Nurseline, PO Box 79251, Royal Heights, Auckland. Tel: 64-9-4644. Fax: 64-9-416 4014.

Panacea Healthcare, PO Box 33 750, Auckland. Tel: 64-9-489 5159.

Health First Network Ltd, PO Box 27048, Christchurch. Tel: 64-3-365 8946. Fax: 64-3-365 8951.

Lampen Healthstaff Ltd, 191 Queen Street, Auckland. Tel: 64-9-357 9800. Website: http://www.lampen.co.nz

Nurse Maude Association, PO Box 36126, Merivale, Christchurch. Tel: 64-3-355 6089; Fax: 64-3-355 2051.

## Industry
In a recent survey published by the Northern Employers and Manufacturers Association, Wellington, the word is that manufacturing is 'humming'. Export sales are up 21 per cent on October 1998. Domestic sales are up 9 per cent and staffing up 10 per cent.

When the Asian economy crashed, it badly affected the Tourism Industry. Tourism is now seen as a new and exciting growth industry, which is expected to chalk up 1.5 million visitors for the year ended 1999, with greater predictions for the future. It accounts for 1 in 12 jobs and is one of New Zealand's largest foreign exchange earners at NZ$3.7 billion, slightly below the Diary Board at NZ$4.8 billion.

## Law
There are always places for good keen applicants, but good qualifications are a necessity. To ascertain that your qualifications

reach New Zealand standards you must apply to the Council of Legal Education, 26 Waring Taylor Street, Wellington. Tel: 64-4-471 1161 (Mr Graham Law); Fax: 64-4-473 3963. Legal vacancies are generally advertised in the newspapers (see above under Automotive mechanical engineers details of New Zealand newspapers) and positions are also advertised by personnel consultants.

*Useful addresses*
Wellington District Law Society, 26 Waring Taylor Street, Wellington. Tel: 64-4-472 8978; Fax: 64-4-471 0375. Email: *wellaw@ wellaw.co.nz*

Auckland District Law Society, PO Box 58, Auckland. Tel: 64-9-303 5270; Fax: 64-9-309 3726. Website: *http://www.adls.org.nz*

## Working in the office environment
The following information was made available to me by the Lampen Group. It was compiled from a summary of findings from the 1999 Lampen Salary Survey.

## Wellington
*Secretarial/word processing*
Skill shortages exist as candidates require more variety and challenge than roles limited to a high WP content. There has been an increase in multiskilling in this area. Finding people interested in straight WP work has become increasingly difficult.

*Reception*
There is a shortage of suitable candidates with appropriate personality, grooming and oral/written communication skills.

*Information Technology*
As this industry develops so rapidly, skill-based training is needed to allow staff to match their skill level to the pace of industry development.

*Accounts*
There is a market perception that accounts roles are 'backroom', yet employers' expectations are that customer services and frontline people skills are required in such roles. There is a shortage of people with CHRIS payroll experience. There is a greater emphasis on people skills for accounting graduates. Accountants have experi-

enced marked salary increases.

*Clerical*
There has been an increase in intermediate to advanced administration roles which include multiple responsibilities, i.e. there is a higher expectation that a PA will complete advanced administration tasks as well as word processing work which requires high computer literacy.

*Marketing and customer service*
These roles are currently very popular. Telemarketing and Telesales are growing rapidly with the increase in customer focus and technology, i.e. the increase in use of 0800 lines (free phones). These roles are replacing sales representatives in some cases.

*Sales*
Many applicants lack an understanding of the sales process, i.e. specialist product knowledge and negotiation skills. Sales salary packages frequently include faxes and mobile phones.

*Graduates*
Are being most frequently employed in legal, policy or human resource roles.

*Legal*
There has been a chronic and consistent shortage of legal secretaries, and many firms are training up secretarial staff into these roles. Skilled legal executives are commanding high salaries. An increase in speech recognition software usage attempts to deal with the increase in OSS/RSI and the emphasis on typing speed as a prerequisite for many roles.

> *Note*: There is a massive skills shortage in the New Zealand employment market. In Wellington it is concentrated in legal, secretarial, technical and payroll CHRIS areas.

**Auckland**
Auckland businesses are currently facing a skill shortage. The skill areas most affected are sales and marketing, secretarial (especially secretaries with legal experience), customer services, accounts and accountants, computer skills and reception skills.

*Skills*
More is now expected from employees in the commercial office area. Often staff will be expected to have more than one skill or to be multi-skilled. Employees themselves also have higher expectations of these roles. They are looking for career development, the opportunity to learn new skills and diversity in their roles. Accordingly salaries have been pushed in an upward direction for these roles. Secretarial, word processing and reception roles have become less defined and more intertwined. Many employees prefer not to perform high word processing content roles, because of the dangers and high incidence of OSS (Occupational Strain Syndrome). It is important for people in these roles to keep in touch with continually changing office technology with training and up-skilling.

Office technology and more sophisticated use of technology has created great demand for systems operators and administrators.

IT and accounts staff, particularly accountants, are in high demand and those with experience are difficult to source.

*Sales staff*
The sales area is one of the most difficult for employers to staff at present. While many people are interested in these roles there are insufficient experienced people available, particularly those who may have specialist technical or industry experience. Demand for qualified marketers has also increased.

Telestaffing (or teleservicing, telemarketing and telesales) is a rapidly growing area of the employment market. There is increased demand for people with training or experience specific to telephone-based work. A sales or customer services background is important to most of these roles. More people are becoming interested in these roles and considering them as career options.

*Opportunities*
In general, the Auckland employment market offers many opportunities to skilled employees. There are plenty of positions available for people who have experience and the right attitude.

## Christchurch
As with the Auckland and Wellington employment markets, the Christchurch employment market is experiencing a severe skill shortage in certain areas. Specifically these are: technical and information technology skills, accounting skills and legal administrative skills.

*Secretarial and clerical*
The Christchurch market currently requires more people with basic experience for general secretarial roles. As in Auckland, many employers prefer roles that offer more diversity and personal challenge than pure secretarial roles, therefore this gap needs to be filled. Again there is an intermingling of secretarial, word processing and reception roles, so that employees receive the diversity and challenge they seek from employment.

There is an insufficient pool of general and specialised clerical candidates to meet the current demand of employers. Many of the roles opening up on this area require basic rather than advanced skills.

*Reception*
Reception roles are increasingly being recognised as important frontline positions where contact with customers is made. Reception staff are expected to have highly developed communication and rapport-building skills.

*Technology*
Rapidly changing office technology has left the Christchurch employment market with a deficit of available employees to cope with change and upgrading technology. This is very evident in all computer-related roles – secretarial, systems operators, accounts and information technology.

*Accountants*
Accountants, both at graduate and more experienced levels, are in demand.

*Sales*
There are many opportunities for sales staff with planning and strategic skills, as well as the right personal attributes to match the culture of the employer company.

*Opportunities*
In general the Christchurch employment market has many opportunities for job-seekers, particularly those with computer related skills.

## Optometrists

There are vacancies for optometrists in New Zealand but they are usually in the lower half of the North Island or in the South Island. Auckland has few vacancies because Auckland University runs the optometry courses, and the students prefer to stay in Auckland when they have qualified. I was told that some of the small urban and out of the way areas have difficulty in recruiting optometrists. Firstly you should contact the NZ Association of Optometrists and they will inform you what qualifications you need to be able to work in New Zealand. They will also answer any questions you may have.

New Zealand Association of Optometrists (Inc), PO Box 1978, Wellington. Tel: 64-4-473 2322; Fax: 64-4-473 2328.

## Professional and technical

(Engineering, Architectural Construction, Scientific, Petro-chemical, Manufacturing, Computing, Sales/Marketing)

There isn't much flexibility in this field of employment as there has in the past been an oversupply of architects, botanists, zoologists, geologists and geneticists flooding out from New Zealand universities.

Row Law Consulting informed me that applicants needed to be fairly rounded in experience with a degree in Engineering (BSc) with 5–7 years run of experience. Where they have had several disciplines covered in that experience, e.g. waste treatment and water supply, they will stand a better opportunity than those who are specialised. Work experience outside the UK is also an advantage as is experience in seismic codes.

*Useful addresses*

New Zealand Institute of Architects Inc, 102–112 Lambton Quay, Wellington. Tel: 64-4-473 5346; Fax: 64-4-472 0182.

Institute of Geological and Nuclear Sciences Ltd, PO Box 30-368, Lower Hutt, Wellington. Tel: 64-4-570 1444; Fax: 64-4-569 0600.

Institution of Professional Engineers New Zealand (IPENZ), PO Box 12–241, Wellington. Tel: 64-4-473 9444; Fax: 64-4-473 2324. Website: *http://www.ipenz.org.nz*

## Pharmacists

All pharmacists who intend working in New Zealand need to contact the Pharmaceutical Society of New Zealand to be registered.

Address: 124 Dixon Street, Wellington. Tel: 64-4-385 9604; Fax: 64-4-382 9297.

There is a huge shortage of pharmacists in New Zealand. A registered pharmacist can expect to earn approximately $26–$30 per hour. There is a four week waiting period, after registration, before you can practise. Initial contact can be made by enquiring at the Provincial Pharmacy Services International office in Birmingham, UK.

*Useful addresses*

NZ Pharmacy, PO Box 99141, Newmarket, Auckland. Fax: 64-9-522 1991.

NZ Pharmacy Employment Ltd, Private Bag, Wairere Road, Auckland 1250. Tel: 64-9-810 9288.

New Zealand Hospital Pharmacists Association, Box 11-640, Wellington. Tel: 64-4-385 9604; Fax: 64-4-382 9297.

The Pharmacy Guild of NZ (Inc), Box 27-139, Wellington. Tel: 64-4-385 9708; Fax: 64-4-384 8085.

**Physiotherapists**

Assessment of qualifications and registration is undertaken by the Physiotherapy Board of New Zealand who assess each application. The assessment process can take between four and six weeks.

The Board administers all forms of physiotherapy registration. Registration is a *legal requirement* for practising physiotherapy in New Zealand. Physiotherapists intending to work in New Zealand must complete formalities for registration *before* taking up employment. Write to the Physiotherapy Board and they will send you the necessary forms and information booklet. You will be required to pay an application fee of NZ$300.00 which is non-refundable.

Jobs can be found by looking in the newspapers and also through contacting New Zealand hospitals. (See above under Health for addresses.)

*Useful addresses*

New Zealand Physiotherapy Board, PO Box 10–140, Wellington. Tel: 64-4-499 7979; Fax: 64-4-472 2350.

New Zealand Society of Physiotherapists, Box 27386, Wellington Tel: 64-4-801 6500; Fax: 64-4-801 5571.

## Podiatrists

All enquiries regarding registration should be made to the Podiatrists Board. Jobs can be found through the newspapers or by contacting the hospitals. (See above under Health for addresses.)

*Useful addresses*
Podiatrists Board, Box 10-140, Wellington. Tel: 64-4-499 7979; Fax: 64-4-472 2350.

## Psychologists

Jobs can be found through contacting the hospitals (see above under Health for addresses) and reading the newspapers for vacancies. Enquiries should be made to the Psychologists Board.

*Useful addresses*
Psychologists Board, Box 10-140, Wellington. Tel: 64-4-499 7979; Fax: 64-4-472 2350.

New Zealand College of Clinical Psychologists, PO Box 28-219, Remuera, Auckland. Tel: 64-9-529 4501.

## Quantity surveyors

There are good opportunities in New Zealand for quantity surveyors. Write direct to the Institute together with a copy of your CV.

*Useful address*
NZ Institute of Quantity Surveyors Inc, 44 The Terrace, Wellington. Tel: 64-4-473 5521. Email: *karl/bale@nziqs.co.nz*

## Real estate agents

You will need to gain a New Zealand registration, and details can be obtained from the Real Estate Institute of NZ (Inc). Jobs can be found by looking in the newspapers in the area of your choice, or by writing to the main agencies in New Zealand.

*Useful addresses*
Real Estate Institute of NZ (Inc), PO Box 1247, Wellington. Tel: 64-4-472 8942; Fax: 64-4-471 2262.

Real Estate Agents:
Harcourts Group Limited, Harcourts Building, Lambton Quay,

Wellington. Tel: 64-4-472 6209. (Harcourts have over 120 offices nationwide.)

Challenge Realty Services Ltd, (L J Hooker), 58–62 Johnsonville Road, Johnsonville, Wellington. Tel: 64-4-478 3109; Fax: 64-4-478 3106. (Offices throughout NZ.)

First National Real Estate, 20 Johnsonville Road, Johnsonville, Wellington. Tel: 64-4-478 1620. (Offices throughout NZ.)

## Valuers

It is necessary for overseas applicants to sit a law paper, and they must have been resident in New Zealand for 12 months. Job opportunities are limited. All applications and enquiries should be made to the New Zealand Institute of Valuers.

*Useful addresses*
Valuers Registration Board, Box 5098, Wellington. Tel: 64-4-471 6331.

NZ Institute of Valuers, PO Box 27-146, Wellington. Tel: 64-4-385 8436; Fax: 64-4-382 9214. Website: *http://www.nziv.org.nz*

## Veterinarians

There are plenty of vacancies for veterinarians in New Zealand. You will need to register with the Veterinary Council of New Zealand. Jobs can be found in the newspapers and also through contacting the Veterinary Association.

*Useful addresses*
Patty Beckenham, Veterinary Association NZ (Inc), PO Box 12147, Christchurch. Tel: 64-3-337 1051.

Veterinary Council of NZ, PO Box 10-563, Wellington. Tel: 64-4-473 9600; Fax: 64-4-473 8869.

## PERSONNEL CONSULTANTS

A.P.S. Personnel, 611 Great South Road, Manukau, Auckland. Tel: 64-9-263 4824. (Engineering, office and secretarial, hotel and leisure staff.)

Accountech Recruitment, 2 Hunter Street, Wellington. Tel: 64-4-499 3322; Fax: 64-4-471 1385. (Finance and banking.)

Adcorp NZ Ltd, for jobs via the web. Website: *http://www.career.co.nz*

Advance Management & Personnel Consultants Limited, 166 Great South Road, Papatoetoe, Auckland South. Tel: 64-9-277 9930. (Senior management, secretarial, accounting, technical, sales/ marketing, administration, engineering.)

Advanced Personnel Services Limited, 829 Colombo Street, Christchurch. Tel: 64-3-365 4322. (Office and secretarial, information and technology staff, executives, engineering, accountants, draughting, design engineers, computer systems/operators, labour hire, builders, tradesmen.)

Alectus Recruitment Consultants Ltd, Box 2186, Wellington. Tel: 64-4-473 4033; Fax: 64-4-498 0548. (Secretarial, reception, administration, promotional, accounts.)

Alpha Personnel Recruitment Limited, PO Box 99 256, Newmarket, Auckland. Tel. 64-9-524 2336; Fax: 64-9-524 2794. (Accounting, sales and marketing, secretarial, clerical, word processing, computer operators, data entry, advertising/media.) Email: *info@alphajobs.co.nz*

Andrews Partners Recruitment, 2 Hunter Street, Wellington. Tel: 64-4-473 333; Fax: 64-4-471 1385. (Computers.)

Cameron Mackay & Ellis, 2 Hunter Street, Wellington. Tel: 64-4-499 6688; Fax: 64-4-499 8665. (Executive and management.)

Candle NZ Ltd, 11 Hunter Street, Wellington. Tel: 64-4-473 9149. Website: *http://www.candlenz.co.nz* (IT recruitment.)

Clayton Ford Consulting Group, PO Box 10–083, Wellington. Tel: 64-4-473 6223; Fax: 64-4-471 2100. (Finance and banking.) Website: *http://www.claytonford.co.nz*

Cooney & Associates, Fujitsu House, 126 The Terrace, Wellington. Tel: 64-4-472 3455; Fax: 64-4-472 3448. (Executive and management.)

Drake International Ltd, Southpac Tower, Queen Street, Auckland. Tel: 64-9-379 5610. Website: *http://www.drakeintl.com* (General office, management, medical, industrial.)

Duncan & Ryan Associates, 135 Victoria Street, Wellington. Tel: 64-4-802 4888; Fax: 64-4-472 7923. Website: *http://www.duncanryan.co.nz* (Computers.)

Hawkins Associates, PO Box 10–013, Wellington. Tel: 64-4-499 9199; Fax: 64-4-472 8620. Email: *hawkins.assoc@xtra.co.nz* (Professional and technical.)

IDPE Consulting Group, 117 Customhouse Quay, Wellington. Tel: 64-4-472 1151; Fax: 64-4-471 1119. Website: *http://idpe-consulting .co.nz* (Computers.)

Kelly Services (NZ) Ltd, 2 Hunter Street, Wellington. Tel: 64-4-499 2825. (Accounting, banking, WP operators, sales, secretarial, management, telemarketing, hospitality, marketing, clerical.)

Kelly Services (NW) Ltd, PO Box 13 418, Christchurch. Tel: 64-3-379 2963. (Secretarial, data entry, WP operators, medical, reception, spreadsheet operators, accounting, legal, sales and marketing, tradespeople, drivers, hospitality.)

Lacey Lee Simpson, PO Box 27144, Wellington. Tel: 64-4-382 9974. Website: *http://www.laceyleesimpson.co.nz* (IT recruitment.)

Lampen Group Limited, PO Box 2438, Auckland. Tel: 64-9-357 9800; Fax: 64-9-357 9801. Website: *http://www.lampen.co.nz*

McLay & Co (NZ) Ltd, PO Box 10–626, Wellington. Tel: 64-4-499 5385; Fax: 64-4-499 1385. (Accountants.)

McLay & Co (NZ) Ltd, PO Box 6798, Wellesley Street, Auckland. Tel: 64-9-302 5340; Fax: 64-9-358 5354. (Accountants.)

Maxim Recruitment Group Ltd, 113–119 The Terrace, Wellington. Tel: 64-4-499 0344. (Secretarial, temps, word processing, computer operating, data entry, management, professional.)

Mercury Consulting Group Ltd, 1 Grey Street, Wellington. Tel: 64-

4-499 2624; Fax: 64-4-499 1655. (IT and computer professionals, telecommunications and electronic engineers.)

Morgan & Banks, PO Box 2186, Wellington. Tel: 64-4-473 4073; Fax: 64-4-472 1171. Website: *http://www.morganbanks.co.au* (Executive and management.)

NZ Pharmacy Employment, Private Bag, Waitakere, Auckland. Tel: 64-9-810 9288. (Pharmacists, technicians, shop assistants.)

Rob Law Consulting Group, PO Box 10080, Wellington. Tel: 64-4-499 8800; Fax: 64-4-499 0955. Email: *roblawauck@clear.net.nz* (Engineering, architectural, construction, scientific, petro-chemical, manufacturing, computing, sales/marketing.)

Rodgers & Partners, PO Box 391, Christchurch. Tel: 64-3-379 8909; Fax: 64-3-365 4494. (Executive and management.)

Select Appointments, 342 Lambton Quay, Wellington. Tel: 64-4-471 0501. (Secretarial, word processing, computer operators, reception.)

Sheffield Consulting Group, PO Box 10-253, Wellington. Tel: 64-4-471 0122; Fax: 64-4-471 0413. Website: *http://www.sheffield.co.nz/ vis.htm* (Finance and banking.)

Staff 'U' Limited, 171 Parnell Road, Parnell, Auckland. Tel: 64-9-377 9605. (Chefs, bar staff, kitchen hands, waitering staff, hospitality industry.)

Stanford Recruitment Consultants, 296 Lambton Quay, Wellington. Tel: 64-4-499 4994. Email: *Stanford.ltd@xtra.co.nz* (PAs, WP operators, admin, finance and accounting.)

The Doughty Group Limited, PO Box 10-234, Wellington. Tel: 64-4-473 9149; Fax: 64-4-472 7932. (Computers.)

Western Staff Services, PO Box 4333, Auckland. Tel: 64-9-309 6685; Fax: 64-9-308 9299. (Senior and middle management, office and clerical, sales and marketing, light industrial.)

Wheeler Campbell Consulting Ltd, 177 Queen Street, Auckland.

Tel: 64-9-303 4500; Fax: 64-9-302 3488. Website: *http://www.wheelercampbell.co.nz* (Professional and technical.)

## MEETING NEW ZEALAND QUALIFICATION REQUIREMENTS

Be kind to yourself – don't take the word of anyone unqualified who says that your qualifications will be alright. Seek assistance from the New Zealand Embassy or Consulate before you leave home, and write to:

New Zealand Qualifications Authority Board, PO Box 160, Wellington. Website: *http://www.nzqa.govt.nz*

Make sure that you have got verification in writing *before* leaving home for distant shores. It is a lot less expensive, time-consuming and heart-breaking.

## CASE STUDIES

### Sally learns the hard way
Sally decided to work in New Zealand for a change of pace. She was a well-qualified physiotherapist and had got tired of the National Health system and the stress it produced. She left Chester almost as soon as she received confirmation that her application for permanent residency had been approved. Upon arrival in Auckland she found that before she could work in New Zealand she had to apply to the Physiotherapy Board for registration. Putting together all the information they required took time, especially as she had left some of her personal possessions with her parents in Manchester and had to get them to post them over to her. It took five weeks for the Registration Board to process her application. It was two months before Sally could commence working, two months of unnecessary stress which could have been avoided if she had found out what was required *before* she left England.

### Keith sticks to the rules
Keith came to New Zealand as a temporary visitor (student category) which permitted him to stay and study for a maximum of four years. He enrolled as a full-time student at a tertiary institution, studying farming.

He supplemented his spending money by working part-time, knowing that he was only allowed to work for up to 15 hours per week, under the terms of his permit. His employer was very pleased with him and asked if he would work more hours. Keith explained that he couldn't because of his work restriction. His employer told him he wouldn't be found out and tried to coerce Keith to change his mind. Keith still refused, and sadly his employment was terminated. However, the following week he was able to find another part-time job for just 15 hours per week.

## The Browning family make a choice

Peter and his family wanted a better environment for their children. Peter was a qualified electronics engineer in Bristol and had worked on radar systems and atomic power stations before turning to computer software in 1970. They moved to New Zealand in 1974 and Peter quickly found a position as a programmer with a large computer payroll organisation. After a number of years he joined a commercial organisation as programming manager. In 1981 he joined a firm of consultants and is now director of the consultancy. He spends time each year recruiting to fill the many assignments they handle. His family have grown and prospered in New Zealand, and now lead an enviable lifestyle which includes trips back 'home' every two years.

## POINTS FOR DISCUSSION

1. Could you afford the expense of having to sit a Medical Council registration exam upon arrival in New Zealand, knowing that it could take several months before you could work?

2. Would you feel slighted at being told that your qualifications were not sufficient for New Zealand?

3. Do you have enough skills other than your qualified position which could support you while you awaited your registration approval if you arrived in New Zealand before it was granted?

# 9

# Retraining

## FINDING TRAINING ASSISTANCE

With the introduction of Skill New Zealand, the artificial divide between 'academic' and 'vocational' education and training is disappearing. The two government agencies responsible for Skill New Zealand are the New Zealand Qualifications Authority and the Education and Training Support Agency. In addition to a number of Skill New Zealand initiatives which aim to foster high quality industry training, the Education and Training Support Agency is responsible for the Training Opportunities Programme, which aims to provide training for long-term unemployed people with low or no qualifications.

## GOING TO UNIVERSITY

There are seven universities in New Zealand. They are the University of Auckland, the University of Waikato, Massey University, Victoria University of Wellington, the University of Canterbury, Lincoln University and the University of Otago.

### Courses

All universities offer courses in the usual faculties of arts, science and commerce, while law and music courses are available at Auckland, Waikato, Victoria, Canterbury and Otago. Most universities specialise in certain fields:

- University of Otago in medicine, dentistry, physical education, pharmacy and surveying.
- University of Canterbury in forestry, engineering and fine arts.
- Lincoln University in topics related to agriculture and horticulture.
- University of Auckland in architecture, planning, engineering,

medicine, optometry and fine arts.

● Victoria University of Wellington in architecture, public administration and social work.

Massey University has courses in agriculture, horticulture, food technology and veterinary science, as well as extra-mural tuition in a wide range of subjects throughout New Zealand. Conjoint programmes leading to the Bachelor of Education degree and Diploma of Teaching are available at several universities in association with local colleges of education.

## Continuing education

All seven universities have centres for continuing education. A typical university education centre has a director-in-charge and a staff of lecturers in a range of academic disciplines. The courses are conducted by various methods – lectures, study conferences, seminars, school of varying lengths (both residential and non-residential) and correspondence courses. Most universities continue to offer the general public substantial continuing education programmes in the liberal studies area. There has been, however, a significant increase in programmes designed for specialist groups, especially occupational. Some of these are national in scope.

*North Island*

University of Auckland, Private Bag 92019, Auckland. Tel: 64-9-373 7513; Fax: 64-9-373 7405. Website: *http://www.auckland.ac.nz*

University of Waikato, Private Bag 3105, Hamilton. Tel: 64-7-856 2889; Fax: 64-7-838 4269. Website: *http://www.waikato.ac.nz*

Massey University, Private Bag 11–122, Palmerston North. Tel: 64-6-356 9099; Fax: 64-6-350 5603. Website: *http://www.massey.ac.nz*

Victoria University of Wellington, Box 600, Wellington. Tel: 64-4-472 1000; Fax: 64-4-499 4601. Website: *http://www.vuw.ac.nz*

*South Island*

Canterbury University, Private Bag 4800, Christchurch. Tel: 64-3-366 7001; Fax: 64-3-364 2999. Website: *http://www.canterbury.ac.nz*

Lincoln University, PO Box 94, Canterbury. Tel: 64-3-325 2811; Fax: 64-3-325 2965. Website: *http://www.lincoln.ac.nz*

Otago University, PO Box 56, Dunedin. Tel: 64-3-479 11–; Fax: 64-3-474 1607. Website: *http://www.otago.ac.nz*

## TRAINING AT A POLYTECHNIC COLLEGE

Over recent decades vocational education and training has moved away from the secondary to the continuing education sector, with training formerly provided by technical high schools now provided for by polytechnics. Polytechnics offer a diverse range of vocational and professional programmes and cover an increasing number of various levels of specialisation.

There are 25 Polytechnics in New Zealand. They are Northland Polytechnic, Unitech-Institute of Technology, Auckland Institute of Technology, Manukau Polytechnic, Waikato Polytechnic, Bay of Plenty Polytechnic, Waiariki Polytechnic, Tairawhiti Polytechnic, Hawke's Bay Polytechnic, Wairarapa Community Polytechnic, Taranaki Polytechnic, Wanganui Regional Polytechnic, Manawatu Polytechnic, Whitireia Polytechnic, Central Institute of Technology, The Open Polytechnic of New Zealand, Hutt Valley Polytechnic, Wellington Polytechnic, Nelson Polytechnic, Tai Poutini Polytechnic, Christchurch Polytechnic, Aoraki Polytechnic, Otago Polytechnic, Telford Polytechnic and Southland Polytechnic. For further details about these organisations write to the Association of Polytechnics in New Zealand, 10344, Wellington.

## CENTRAL INSTITUTE OF TECHNOLOGY (CIT)

Over 5,000 students a year from all over New Zealand go to the Central Institute of Technology to study the wide range of courses offered. Most courses fall into the areas of health and science, management or engineering, including many unique sources such as dental technology, podiatry, computer and software engineering, interior design, medical radiation therapy and embalming and funeral directing. An international flavour is added to the campus by CITEC Training Solutions, a wholly-owned subsidiary of CIT that manages training programmes for overseas students, some coming from as far away as Hong Kong, Switzerland and Pakistan.

A variety of qualifications are offered including bachelor degrees, diplomas, awards, certificates and New Zealand certificates. Studies can take from a few weeks to four years full-time study. Most courses are available to school-leavers, although some educational prerequisites are required for some courses.

*Note*: Experienced professional people can acquire new skills at intensive short courses and seminars, and people seeking 'second chance' education can enrol in foundation or 'bridging' courses leading to either employment or further study.

The campus is located in Heretaunga in Upper Hutt, Wellington. For further information write to:

Central Institute of Technology, Somme Road, Heretaunga, Upper Hutt, Wellington. Tel: 64-4-527 6398; Fax: 64-4-527 6359.

## ADVANCED VOCATIONAL AWARDS AND TRADE CERTIFICATION BOARD EXAMINATIONS

The New Zealand Qualifications Authority has responsibility for Trade Certification and Advanced Vocational Awards, including the curriculum and examination of all three-stage technician certificates, five-stage New Zealand Certificate Courses and the examination of candidates sitting trade certificate or advanced trade certification qualifications. The New Zealand Diploma offers an advanced qualification for students who have completed a New Zealand Certificate in the same or a related area.

### Attending technician courses

Both the five-year New Zealand Certificate and the three-year technician certificate are offered in a variety of vocational areas. New Zealand Certificate courses are part-time and require regular study at day-release and evening classes or intermittent periods of full-time study block courses.

Most subjects may be studied through the Open Polytechnic of New Zealand. Students may also study selected New Zealand Certificate courses full-time at a polytechnic. All New Zealand Certificates require students to complete not less than three years of suitable work experience.

### Attending trade courses

Training for trade qualifications account for a significant percentage of the work of polytechnics. The New Zealand Qualifications Authority has approved a wide range of trade courses and prescriptions under which assessment, examination and certification are conducted. Education and training requirements for the various trades are listed in the respective prescriptions. They specify a mix of theory and practical training, to be obtained through education providers and through on-job experience. The completion of prescribed requirements leads to the issue of Trade Certificate and Advanced Trade Certificate qualifications.

## CASE STUDIES

### Duncan finds a way
Duncan had served his apprenticeship as a fitter welder. He had never considered any other form of employment. After straining his back he found the work aggravated the injury. He applied to a firm who regularly supplied his workshop with tools and was successful in becoming their sales representative for the Auckland area. Duncan was lucky in that he didn't need to retrain because his acquired skills plus sales training enabled him to become a first class representative.

### Louise uses her skills
After four years at Auckland University Louise qualified as a musician. Unfortunately she was unable to find full-time employment. In her final year at College she had achieved top marks in maths. This had always been a strong subject for her, so she was able to find work as a part-time bank teller. Thus she spent half her week teaching music and the other half working in the bank.

### Peter changes his approach
Peter trained as a surveyor and found work as soon as his training was complete. He was also a very good and keen golfer. Golf finally overtook his job as a surveyor, and he became a semi-professional with plans to be a professional within two years. When he was involved in a road accident and his ankle was broken, he knew that he would no longer to able to proceed as a professional golfer and he had to think about his future. He now has a very successful business introducing overseas visitors to the golf courses in New Zealand he even does some coaching.

## POINTS FOR DISCUSSION

1. Would you be prepared to retrain to fill a demand?

2. Would you consider becoming multi-skilled?

3. Would you consider having two different part-time jobs?

# 10

## Understanding the New Zealand Health Structure

The New Zealand health system is made up of public, private and voluntary sectors which interact to provide and fund health care. Over 70 per cent of health care is publicly funded.

### MINISTRY OF HEALTH

The Ministry is the government's chief adviser and monitoring agent for health and disability services. Its functions include strategic planning; health policy advice; review; specification and assessment of services; regulation and health protection; and the management of health funding.

### REGIONAL HEALTH AUTHORITIES

There are four regional health authorities (RHAs) and they are responsible for purchasing health and disability services for New Zealanders. RHAs also manage contracts with service providers, specifying the services being provided. The four authorities are:

- North Health (Auckland)

- Midland Regional Health Authority (Hamilton)

- Central Regional Health Authority (Wellington)

- Southern Regional Health Authority (Dunedin).

The RHAs contract with organisations such as Crown Health Enterprises (CHEs), private hospitals and individuals such as doctors to purchase health care for all those who need it. The integration of funding will give incentives for more effective use of resources. RHAs seek the best possible standard of health care, at the best possible price, and have the option of purchasing health care from the public, private or voluntary sectors.

## CROWN HEALTH ENTERPRISES (HOSPITALS)

There are 23 Crown Health Enterprises and they come under the umbrella of the regional health authority in their region. Individual Crown Health Enterprises generally provide health care and disability services for a particular area based around a 24-hour acute care tertiary (high technology) hospital.

## GETTING DENTAL CARE

New Zealand's dental health service combines a school dental service for children, dental benefits for adolescents and private practice for adults. Major hospitals also provide dental services for in-patients, students and people on low incomes. Children who remain in full-time study after age 16 continue to receive dental benefits up to age 18.

Adults have to pay for their own dental treatment, and it doesn't come cheap!

| Procedure | Typical fee |
|---|---|
| Examination, X-ray and polish | $60 |
| Normal filling | $60/$120.00 |
| Root filling | $60/$200.00 |

The cost of having all your teeth removed and dentures fitted is also costly, anything from $2,000.

## APPLYING FOR ACCIDENT COMPENSATION

In New Zealand no one has the right to sue (in any court) for damages (apart from exemplary damages) for personal injuries that are covered by ACC.

A comprehensive system of accident rehabilitation and compensation insurance is provided for all New Zealanders under the Accident Rehabilitation and Compensation Insurance Act 1992. The Act has an emphasis on injury prevention, rehabilitation, risk management and compensation. It specifically acknowledges that risk management and rehabilitation are facets of injury and compensation cost control and that injury prevention, rehabilitation, risk management and compensation strategies need to be integrated.

## Provisions for visitors

If you are visiting New Zealand and are hurt in a work or motor vehicle accident while here, the costs of treatment provided by the hospital will be paid for you. Provided you meet some eligibility criteria, ACC is also able to pay for a range of other services up to limits defined in regulations. For example, visits to a general practitioner, physiotherapy, provision of home help and weekly compensation (where applicable).

Unless you are covered by a reciprocal health agreement (that is, you are a UK national or an Australian resident), if you are involved in an accident that is not work or motor vehicle related (for example, sports injuries or accidents at home), you may need to pay for some of these services yourself, either in part or in full. For some difficult types of claims, it can take some time to establish cover under the scheme. In these cases you may need to pay for the services initially and seek reimbursement from ACC once cover has been established. For many services, ACC will not be able to make full payments, which means that you will be responsible for paying any difference. Exact entitlements are determined on a case by case basis.

## Taking out insurance

Taking out private travel/medical insurance is the best way to be certain you are able to pay for any extra health costs you may face should you be injured while visiting New Zealand.

## HEALTH CARE FOR LONG-TERM VISITORS

Anyone who has a valid permit to be in New Zealand and can prove an intention to stay for two or more years, also has access to the full range of health care services on the same basis as New Zealand citizens or permanent residents. This includes students enrolled in courses lasting two or more years and people with long-term work contracts.

## HEALTH CARE FOR SHORT-TERM VISITORS

If you are intending to visit New Zealand for a short period of time, whether for work or a holiday, the Ministry of Health advises you to get travel/medical insurance before leaving home. It is recommended that you get travel/medical insurance that will cover the cost of emergency services and hospital care while in New Zealand. It is important to check with your travel agent or insurance company exactly what costs your medical insurance covers, *before* you leave home.

## COVERING YOURSELF WITH MEDICAL INSURANCE

It is advisable to check out the range of cover offered by medical insurers. If you specifically want dental cover you must ensure that the insurer of your choice covers this, as dental care is not covered by all medical insurers. It is also wise to ensure that emergencies requiring hospital treatment are well covered, e.g. heart surgery and other major surgery. Medical insurance is quite competitive in New Zealand and it would pay you to check out what is available before deciding which insurer you should use.

### Useful addresses
The following insurers have offices throughout New Zealand:

Aetna Health (NZ) Ltd, 57 Courtenay Place, Te Aro, Wellington. Tel: 64-4-384 5767.

Medic Aid, Private Bag 92082, Auckland. Tel: 64-9-307 2915; Fax: 64-9-303 0468.

Medic Aid (Head Office), Private Bag 3056, Hamilton. Tel: 64-7-839 4477; Fax: 64-7-834 2173.

Southern Cross Healthcare (Head Office), Private Bag 99934, Newmarket, Auckland. Tel: 64-9-377 5509.

Southern Cross Healthcare, 171 Vivian Street, Wellington. Tel: 64-4-384 4199; Fax: 64-4-4385 0771.

## Approximate cost of operations

| | |
|---|---|
| Cataracts | $3,200 |
| Tonsils and adenoids (child) | $1,116 |
| (adult) | $1,300 |
| Haemorrhoids | $2,077 |
| Knee replacement | $9,229 |
| Ingrown toenails | $1,122 |
| Mastectomy | $4,700 |
| Cardiac catheterisation | $2,800 |
| Hip replacement | $9,500 |
| Hysterectomy | $3,600 |

## CASE STUDIES

### Marie learns the hard way

Marie didn't have time to have her teeth checked before she left England for New Zealand. After several months of living and working in Auckland she started to have toothache. Upon enquiring she discovered that dental care was not covered by a health scheme in New Zealand. The dentist told her that her fillings were deep and she would need root canal fillings which was a rather lengthy and expensive process. She had no choice but to agree and learnt her lesson the hard way when she was presented with a bill for $300 for each root canal filling.

### John and Sue pay up

John, Sue and their small daughter Elizabeth had been living in New Zealand for two years. They had managed to find jobs and had even budgeted for their own home. Elizabeth had been getting sore throats since she started school six months previously. As time went by they got worse. The doctor advised them that she needed her tonsils removed. They agreed with his decision and found that they would have to wait for 12 months as there was a long waiting list. Fortunately they had made private health care a priority and joined a health insurance plan. Upon advising the company of their plight they received an application form which they quickly filled in attaching the specialist's letter of recommendation and within two weeks Elizabeth had been operated on and the health insurance company had paid 80 per cent of the costs.

## Russell has an accident

Russell fell into a hole left uncovered by road workers. It was a dark night and it had been raining and as he walked along the pavement he didn't see the hole because it was unmarked. He fell onto his knees and was badly grazed. He went to the doctor who filled in the necessary Accident Compensation claim forms. ACC paid for his doctor's costs and also for physiotherapy treatment. Russell could not sue the contractors for his injury even though he now has permanent damage to his knee, as the ACC scheme does not give anyone the right to sue for personal injury. Russell is now unable to play golf as often as he wishes.

## POINTS FOR DISCUSSION

1. Could you come to terms with the ACC rules?

2. Would you consider private insurance a priority?

3. There is no free dental cover for adults in New Zealand. Could you budget for this expensive treatment?

# 11

## Summing Up

Working in New Zealand has many advantages in that everyone speaks the same language – English. There are cultural differences but they can also be found just by moving around the different parts of Great Britain.

Make out a checklist of the advantages and disadvantages of a move across the other side of the world.

**ADVANTAGES**

- Slower pace of life
- English language
- Less pollution
- No overcrowding
- No terrorism
- A non-nuclear country
- Wide open spaces.

Add your personal advantages:

- 
- 
- 
- 

**DISADVANTAGES**

- Isolation from Europe
- Parochial attitude

- Limited emphasis on the arts
- Over-emphasis on things Maori

Add your personal disadvantages:

•

•

•

•

## CHECKLIST FOR ACTION

1. Start your familiarisation by reading as much as possible about New Zealand.

2. Decide which climate and city you prefer and make your choice accordingly, combining the best place for you to find employment in your particular field.

3. Arrange to receive the New Zealand newspapers and learn about the everyday happenings in New Zealand.

4. Contact the personnel consultants listed in this book and find out about the job opportunities.

5. Contact the New Zealand Embassy in London and get as much information from them as possible.

6. Keep asking questions. Your final decision will then be based on as much information as possible.

7. If you can afford to, travel to New Zealand on a visit first to see if you like the country.

8. If you are not sure if you will like New Zealand, travel light and leave your furnishing in store in England until you are certain you want to live in New Zealand for a period of time. It's much cheaper than giving your furniture a world trip!

9. Before leaving home take the time to build up a list of contacts – friends, relations and distant relatives who could provide a bed for a time.

# Appendix

## EMPLOYMENT AGENCIES

### Auckland

Aacorn International Ltd, PO Box 105-355 Auckland Central. Tel: 09 309 7862. Fax: 09 309 9043. Email: *aacorn@aacorn.co.nz* Website: *www.aacorn.co.nz* Specialising in computer recruitment.

APS Personnel, 611 Great South Road, Manukau. Tel: 09 263 4322 or call free 0800 654 322. Fax: 09 263 4824. Deals with temporary and permanent labour hire (tradesmen, engineering, etc.) office and secretarial staff, hotel and leisure staff and executive leasing.

A & S Consultants International Ltd, 10 Montel Avenue, PO Box 21-761, Henderson. Tel: 09 837 4220. Fax: 09 837 0842. Specialising in technical recruitment: engineers, draftsmen and architects. Permanent and temporary placements catered for.

Accountant Recruitment Limited, PO Box 7209, Wellesley Street, Auckland. Tel: 09 309 2623. Specialists in the placement of temporary accountants and financial executives.

Acorn Healthlink, Suite 1, Level 1, 72 Dominion Road, Auckland. Tel: 09 630 8300.

Ad People, NZ Post Building, 51 Hurstmere Road, Takapuna. Tel: 09 486 1922. Specialising in permanent placements and temporary personnel for advertising agencies and associated industries.

Alectus Recruitment Consultants Ltd, Hewlett Packard House, Quay Street, Auckland. Tel: 09 366 3866. Email: *contactus@ alectus.co.nz* Specialists in secretarial, reception, administration, promotional and accounts recruitment.

Allied Workforce, 41 Station Road, PO Box 12-832, Penrose. Tel: 09 579 0225. Auckland-wide specialists in temporary personnel.

Alpha Personnel Recruitment Ltd, Level 3, 27 Gillies Avenue, PO Box 99-256, Newmarket. Tel: 09 524 2336. Specialising in office staff recruitment together with career counselling, software crosstraining, salary surveys, outplacement, staff assessment, training needs and résumé preparation.

Arrow Personnel Ltd, 136 Queens Road, Panmure, Auckland. Tel: 09 570 2135. Specialist suppliers of temporary and permanent staff.

Ascent Supported Employment, 114-116 Ponsonby Road, Ponsonby, Auckland. Tel: 09 361 1154. Fax: 09 361 1187.

Auckland Medical Bureau, PO Box 37-753, Parnell. Tel: 09 377 5903. For nationwide GP and hospital locums.

Automotive & Technical Personnel Ltd, 2-4 Cain Road, PO Box 112-164, Penrose, Auckland. Tel: 09 579 3200. Fax: 09 579 3700. Email: *cv@autojobs.co.nz* Specialising in motor industry recruitment - sales, technical, parts, administration and management, automotive, heavy automotive and heavy equipment.

Banking Personnel Ltd, West Plaza Building, corner of Albert and Customs Street West, Auckland. Tel: 09 358 0888.

Bridge Personnel and Management Consultants Ltd, PO Box 89-043, Torbay, Auckland. Tel: 09 473 0621.

Centacom Staff Ltd, 31 Dean Street, Grey Lynn, Auckland. Tel: 09 360 2455. Fax: 09 360 1027.

Central Farm Employment, RD 1,Tukau. Tel: 09 233 4885.

Clayton Ford Ltd, Level 16, Westpac Trust Tower, 120 Albert Street, Auckland. Tel: 09 379 9924. Fax: 09 379 7785. Website: *www.claytonford.co.nz* Handles finance, banking and accountancy recruitment.

Credit Control Co Ltd, PO Box 28-196, Auckland. Permanent and temporary employment in office and accounting (Tel: 09 524 2003) sales and marketing (Tel: 09 520 4292) executive and management (Tel: 09 524 7766).

Drake International, 7th Floor, Tower Centre, corner of Queen and Customs Streets, Auckland. Tel: 09 379 5610. Specialises in general office, management, medical and industrial positions either temporary, permanent or contract. Also offers advice and assessment on career moves.

Enterprise Staff Consultants NZ Ltd, Third Level, The Ferry Building, 99 Quay Street, PO Box 1799, Auckland. Tel: 09 306 2160.

Flavell Personnel Consultants, Level 7, Harbour View Building, 152 Quay Street, Auckland. Tel: 09 300 9464. Fax: 09 307 0385.

Gaulter Russell (NZ) Ltd, Level 3, 128 Broadway, Newmarket, PO Box 37-557, Parnell, Auckland. Tel: 09 529 2334.

Hendriks Human Resources, PO Box 105-244, Auckland. Tel: 09 302 3003 or call free 0800 220089. Fax: 09 375 3563. Email:

122 Getting a Job in New Zealand

*service@hendriks.co.nz* Website: *www.hendriks.co.nz*
Horizon Personnel, PO Box 109-711, Newmarket. Tel: 09 379 9899.
Specialises in office support, secretarial, customer services,
accounting, sales/marketing, management and creative recruit-
ment.
Job Connections, Level 3, AMI Building, Osterley Way, Manukau.
Tel: 09 263 6884. Provides employment services for people with
disabilities.
Job Search NZ, PO Box 38-880, Howick, Auckland. Tel: 09 534
1961. Helps with résumés and identification of jobs to match both
ability and requirements.
KC Temps Ltd, Level 17, Metro Media House, 5-7 Byron Avenue,
Takapuna. Tel: 09 486 4796. Fax: 09 486 5207.
Kelly Services, Bridgecorp House, Level 5, 36 Kitchener Street, PO
Box 5393, Wellesley Street, Auckland. Tel: 09 303 3122. Fax: 09
366 7097. Email: *auckland@kellyservices.co.nz* Provides training
and employment opportunities for temporary and permanent
office and industrial placements. No unsolicited CV's.
Lampen Group Limited, Level 16, Telstra Business Centre, 191
Queen Street, PO Box 2438, Auckland. Tel: 09 357 9800. Fax: 09
357 9800. Specialises in technical and office recruitment and
provides consulting services, including psychological assessments
and career counselling.
Law Staff (NZ) Ltd, 11th floor, Price Waterhouse Coopers, 66
Wyndham Street West, Auckland. Tel: 09 377 2248.
Legal and Corporate Staff Ltd, 11th Floor, Price Waterhouse
Coopers, 66 Wyndham Street West, Auckland. Tel: 09 377 1236.
New Zealand Employment Service, Three Kings Plaza, 536 Mount
Albert Road, PO Box 27-203, Auckland. Tel: 09 624 2042. Fax: 09
629 3229.
OPAL Consulting Group, Level 13, Westpac Tower, 120 Albert
Street, PO Box 7067, Auckland. Tel: 09 379 0200. Fax: 09 377
4127. Email: *opal@opal.co.nz* Website: *www.opal.co.nz* OPAL is a
full service recruitment consultancy.
Progressive Personnel Ltd, 40 Eden Crescent, Auckland. Tel: 09 307
6413. Fax: 09 528 6945.
Quinn Staff Recruiters Ltd, Level 7, Landmark House, 187 Queen
Street. Tel: 09 309 8821. Fax: 09 309 8364. Email: *recruit@
quinnstaff.co.nz*
Reed Recruitment Ltd, 100 Anzac Avenue, Auckland. Tel: 09 915
8900 Fax: 09 915 8915. Email: *respond@reedrecruitment.co.nz*
Website: *www.reedrecruitment.co.nz* Human resources specialists

dealing with temporary, permanent and contract employment in accounting, administration, computing, engineering, executive, industrial, management, marketing, reception, sales, secretarial and technical posts.

Schofield Services, 535 Riddell Road, Glendowie. Tel: 09 575 7732. Specialists in accounting placements.

Select Appointments, Level 7, Lufthansa House, 36 Kitchener Street. Tel: 09 307 2042.

Student Job Search, Auckland Institute of Technology, PO Box 5418 Wellesley Street, Auckland. Tel: 09 309 7800. For part time jobs all year and full time summer jobs – no agency fee.

Tempforce, Level 25, ASB Bank Centre, 135 Albert Street, Auckland. Tel: 09 379 2308 or call free 0508 836 736. Fax: 09 379 2307.

The Career Centre, Private Bag 92006, Auckland. Tel: 09 307 9899. Email: *career@ait.ac.nz*

Travel Personnel Ltd, PO Box 28-463, Remeura, Auckland. Tel: 09 520 4291. Fax: 09 520 4237.

Triangle Recruitment Ltd, 235 Broadway, Newmarket. Tel: 09 520 5102.

Walbrook Appointments Ltd, 123 Manakau Road, Epsom. Tel: 09 623 1414. Fax: 09 623 1714.

Westaff, Head Office, Level 2, Emcon House, 75 Queen Street, PO Box 863, Aukland. Tel: 09 356 6904 or call free: 0800 436 756. Fax: 09 356 6905 Email: *headoffice@westaff.co.nz* All levels of recruitment, permanent, temporary and contract.

### Christchurch

Advanced Personnel Services Ltd, Ist Floor, 829 Colombo Street, PO Box 21-348, Christchurch. Tel: 03 365 4322 or call free 0800 365 4322. Fax: 03 365 7356. Email: *enquiries@advanced personnel.co.nz* Website: *www.advancedpersonnel.co.nz* Handles vacancies for office and secretarial staff, information and technology staff, building trades people, store people, labourers, drivers, receptionists, accountants, draughting, design engineers and engineering and hospitality staff.

Drake International Ltd, ANZ Chambers, 160 Cashel Street, Christchurch. Tel: 03 379 5940. Handles vacancies for general office and sales staff and industrial, secretarial, production, administration, accounting, distribution, process and stores staff. Also drivers and labourers for all trades.

Kelly Services (NZ) Ltd, Level 10, Price Waterhouse Centre, 119

Armagh Street, Christchurch. Tel: 03 379 2963. Handles vacancies for secretarial, hospitality and medical staff, data entry, WP operators and receptionists, spreadsheet operators, accounting, clerical, sales and marketing, legal, labourers, truck and van drivers, trades people, mobile plant operators, warehouse staff and process workers.

Lampen Group Ltd, $9^{th}$ floor, NZI Building, 96 Hereford Street, PO Box 3790, Christchurch. Tel: 03 374 9222. Fax: 03 374 9223. Website: www.lampen.co.nz Permanent, contract and temporary staff in office based positions specialising in call centre and customer service.

Mature Employment Service, 199 Armagh Street, Christchurch. Tel: 03 366 4527. Fax: 03 366 6670.

Methven Personnel Consultants Ltd, Level 10, BNZ Building, 137 Armagh Street, Christchurch. Tel: 03 366 5745. Email: enquiry@methven.co.nz

New Zealand Employment Service, 54 Cass Street, PO Box 57, Ashburton. Tel: 0800 559 009. Fax: 03 308 1560. Also 231 High Street, PO Box 22-495, Christchurch. Tel: 03 365 3133. Fax: 03 366 4283.

Workbridge Inc, corner of Durham and Armagh Streets, Christchurch. Tel: 03 377 2188. Specialises in employment and training for people with disabilities.

## Wellington

Accountech Recruitment, ASB Tower, 2 Hunter Street, Wellington. Tel: 04 499 3322.

Ace Personnel, 14 Laings Road, Lower Hutt. Tel: 04 570 0848.

AIESEC New Zealand Inc, PO Box 11-126, Manners Street, Wellington. Tel: 04 499 6480.

Alectus Recruitment Consultants, BNZ Centre, 1 Willis Street, Wellington. Tel: 04 473 4033.

Andersen Contracting, Level 11, Westpac Trust Centre, 125 The Terrace, Wellington. Tel: 04 471 1530. Fax: 04 471 1585. Website: www.swcontracting.com.au

Andrews Partners Recruitment, Level 7, ASB Bank Tower, 2 Hunter Street, Wellington. Tel: 04 473 3333.

Appointments Personnel (Wellington) Ltd, Personal Consultants, Level 9, 34-42 Manners Street, Welllington. Tel: 04 473 5793.

AudDi Recruitment, Level 1, AudDi House, corner of Margaret Street and Queens Drive, Lower Hutt. Tel: 04 570 6611.

Careering Options Ltd, 297 Cuba Street, PO Box 27-020,

Wellington. Tel: 04 384 4200.

CCI NZ Ltd, PO Box 5497, Wellington. Tel: 04 473 8597. Fax: 04 473 7991._ Handles recruitment of professionals in information technology.

Centre Consulting Group, Level 3, AMP Chambers, 187 Featherston Street, Wellington. Tel: 04 473 6833.

Challenger Personnel, 1st Floor, 45 Buick Street, Petone, Lower Hutt. Tel: 04 568 2982. Fax: 04 568 2984.

Clayton Ford Limited, Level 6, Clayton Ford House, 132 The Terrace, Wellington. Tel: 04 473 6223. Fax: 04 471 2100. Web: *www.claytonford.co.nz* Email: *wellington@claytonford.co.nz* Handles finance, banking and accountancy recruitment.

Cooney and Associates, 105 The Terrace, Wellington. Tel: 04 472 3455.

Drake International, Exchange Place, 5-7 Willeston Street, Wellington. Tel: 04 472 6972. Fax: 04 473 4930. Also at Drake House, 72 Queens Drive, Lower Hutt. Tel: 04 569 8876. Fax: 04 569 6104.

GBL Personnel Ltd, 256 Lambton Quay, PO Box 10-435, Wellington. Tel: 04 472 0140. Fax: 04 499 1619. Email: *mailbox@gbl.co.nz* Handles temporary and permanent recruitment of secretarial and office support.

Hawkins Associates, Level 7, 26 Brandon Street, Wellington. Tel: 04 499 9199. Fax: 04 472 8620. Handles vacancies in accounting and finance, information technology, human resources/payroll and administration/secretarial.

Hutt Valley Personnel, AA Centre, Level 2, 29 Waterloo Road, Lower Hutt. Tel: 04 569 5648. Fax: 04 566 4436.

Interchange Corporation Ltd, PO Box 9965, Marion Square, Wellington. Tel: 04 389 6482.

Kelleher Consulting Group, 8/138 The Terrace, Wellington. Tel: 04 473 9094. Handles both temporary and permanent recruitment.

Kelly Services (NZ) Ltd, Level 14, ASB Tower, 2 Hunter Street, Wellington. Tel: 04 499 2825. Also at Level 1, Westpac Building, 8 Margaret Street, Lower Hutt. Tel: 04 569 5200. Website: *www.nzjobs.co.nz*

Lampen Group Limited, Level 2, 107 Custom House Quay, Wellington. Tel: 04 472 4157. Fax: 04 471 0958. Website: *www.lampen.co.nz*

Match 2 Recruitment, ISP Centre, 14 Laings Road, Lower Hutt. Tel: 04 570 0199. Email: *cv@match2.co.nz* Handles vacancies in engineering, science, sales, management and manufacturing.

Mature Employment Support Hutt, 72 Queens Drive, Lower Hutt.

Tel: 04 566 9778.

Maxim Recruitment Group Limited, Level 3, 40 Johnston Street, PO Box 10-516. Tel: 04 499 0344. Fax: 04 499 0350. Email: *maxim@maximgroup.co.nz*

Mercury Consulting Group, Level 9, AMP Centre, 1 Grey Street, PO Box 10-605, Wellington. Tel: 04 499 2624. Specialists in recruiting IT and computer professionals and telecommunications and electronic engineers.

Mid City Personnel Ltd, Terrace Plaza, Level 105, The Terrace, Wellington. Tel: 04 472 5281.

New Zealand Employment Service, Ballantrae House, 192 Willis Street, PO Box 9340, Wellington. Tel: 04 801 9900. Fax: 04 385 4797.

Opal Consulting Group, PO Box 2209, Wellington. Tel: 04 385 4011. Fax: 04 385 6704. Email: *opal@wgtn.opal.co.nz* Website: *www.opal.co.nz*

Paxus People, 80 Boulcott Street, Wellington. Tel: 04 495 4001. Fax: 04 495 4011.

Quin Workforce Ltd, PO Box 45-044, Wellington. Tel: 04 471 0605. Fax: 04 471 0606.

Rob Law Consulting Group Ltd, 105 The Terrace, PO Box 10-080, Wellington. Tel: 04 499 8800. Website: *www.roblaw.co.nz* Specialising in technical personnel, both permanent and contract.

Select Appointments, NCR House, 342 Lambton Quay, PO Box 3651, Wellington. Tel: 04 471 0501. Fax: 04 472 0715.

Stanford Recruitment Consultants Ltd, Level 2, James Cook Arcade, 296 Lambton Quay, PO Box 1505. Tel: 04 472 0861. Fax: 04 499 4994. Permanent and temporary work in corporate market, all areas of support, accounting/finance, etc.

Stewart; K P and Associates, 15 The Masthead, Whitby. Tel: 04 234 8226.

Temp Centre, Level 3, AMP Chambers, 187 Featherston Street, Wellington. Tel: 04 473 6833.

Wellington Student Job Search, Student Union Building, Kelburn Parade, Kelburn, PO Box 9193, Wellington. Tel: 04 472 8105. Fax: 04 471 1181. A professional service specialising in the selection of students for employment during vacation periods and throughout the year. No referral fee.

Westaff, Level 8, Landcorp House, 101 Lambton Quay, PO Box 5188, Wellington. Tel: 04 473 4361. Fax: 04 499 0261. Email: *wellington@westaff.co.nz* All levels of recruitment, permanent, temporary and contract.

## EMPLOYMENT CONTRACT NEGOTIATORS

### Auckland

Arbitration and Alternative Dispute Resolution Centre (NZ) Ltd, PO Box 9166, Newmarket. Tel: 09 638 9995 or call free 0800 ARBITERS.

Bowerman; Clinton N, 9/47 High Street, Auckland. Tel: 09 366 0131. Licensed investigator for all personal grievance disputes and contract negotiation.

Brian Spong and Associates, PO Box 25-351, St. Heliers, Auckland. Tel: 09 575 7301. Free initial telephone conversation for personal grievances, holiday pay advice, mediation, negotiation, employment contract preparation, redundancies, employment tribunal representation and dismissals.

Dean J Organ and Associates Limited, 20 Puriri Avenue, Greenlane, Auckland. Tel: 09 520 4948. Employment solutions consultancy dealing with advocacy, personal grievances, employment relations advice and arbitration.

Employment and Manufacturers Association (Northern) Inc, 159 Khyber Pass Road, Grafton, Auckland. Tel: 09 367 0900. Fax: 09 367 0904. Email: *ema@ema.co.nz* Employment relations consultancy for employers.

Employment Disputes and Dismissal Compensation Services, 80 Anzac Avenue, PO Box 2205, Auckland. Tel: 09 358 2929. Fax: 09 385 5325. Deals with unfair dismissals, redundancies, wage arrears and representation.

Employment Dispute Consultancy, 2/131a Manuka Road, Glenfield. Tel/Fax: 09 444 2733. Email: *disputes@ihug.co.nz* Offers professional advice and representation for employees and employers with personal grievances, disputes, contract drafting and negotiation.

Employment Relations and Advocacy Services Ltd, Level 7/17 Albert Street, Auckland. Tel: 09 377 6510. Fax: 09 358 5325. Deals with personal grievances and employment contracts.

Industrial Conciliation and Mediation Services, PO Box 90-362, Auckland. Tel: 09 443 6454.

Peploe Gregory LLB, Industrial Relations, Level 7/17 Albert Street, Auckland. Tel: 09 302 3920.

## Christchurch

Phil Butler & Associates, Cashel Chambers, 224 Cashel Street, Christchurch. Tel: 03 365 2150. Fax: 03 366 4141. E-mail: *phil.butler@xtra.co.nz* Specialising in employment contract design and negotiations, mediation, personal grievances, employment tribunal advocacy.

Cheyne; Philip, 3 Armagh Court, 78 Armagh Street, Christchurch. Tel: 03 379 5718. Specialist advocates in employment law matters.

Gough Irving Rotherham, 137 Hereford Street, Christchurch. Tel: 03 366 8751. Fax: 03 365 2388. E-mail: *email@gir_law.co.nz* For help with wrongful dismissal and other employment contract problems.

Thompson Logue Associates, 1/78 Armagh Street, Christchurch. Tel: 03 379 4288. Specialists in employment contract advice, advocacy, representation and dispute resolution.

## Wellington

Bargaining Agents, 68 Queens Drive, Lower Hutt, PO Box 31-496. Tel: 04 566 8923. Specialising in labour relations and employment related matter, including safety, health and welfare.

Employers and Manufacturers Association (Central) Inc, 95-99 Molesworth Street, Thorndon, PO Box 1087. Tel: 04 473 7224. Fax: 04 473 4501.

Employment Contract Services Ltd, Wakefield House, 90 The Terrace, Wellington. Tel: 04 471 1720. Fax: 04 473 7495.

Jamieson Partners, 30-32 Mahina Road, Lower Hutt. Tel/Fax: 04 562 7231. Specialises in employment law and tribunal advocacy.

Keenan Consulting, 146a Karori Road, Karori. Tel/Fax: 04 476 6630. Specialists in developing employment contracts, performance agreements, remuneration systems and the related information systems.

## IMMIGRATION CONSULTANTS

### Auckland

AIC Immigration Consultancy (AUCK) Ltd, Dilworth Building, Level 2, corner of Queen and Customs Streets. Tel: 09 302 2091. Fax: 09 302 2096. E-mail: *105312.672@compuserve.com* Specialises in all aspects of immigration including business immigration, points system, family, citizenship, investments, property and employment.

Dorchester and Smythe Ltd, Level 11, Tower 2, The Shortland Centre, 55-65 Shortland Street, Auckland. Tel: 09 377 0616.

Excellence Consultancy Group, 87 Albert Street, Auckland. Tel: 09 377 9338.

Fay Pryor Immigration Services, Level 3, MDC House, 142 Broadway, Newmarket. Tel: 09 529 2745.

Global Immigration Services (NZ) Ltd, 10 New North Road, Eden Terrace, Auckland. Tel: 09 307 6988.

Harder; Christopher, 40 Kingston Street, Auckland. Tel: 09 377 8440. Fax: 09 377 8454. Deals with all immigration related problems including business and work permits, permanent residency, applications and appeals.

Herne Bay Law, 128 Jervois Road, Herne Bay. Tel: 09 378 0511.

International Immigration Consultants, 3/37 Totara Avenue, New Lynn, Auckland. Tel: 09 827 1722.

Kermani Consultants Ltd, Level 7, 17 Albert Street, Auckland. Tel: 09 307 3123.

Legget IBIS International Limited, 401 Queen Street, Auckland. Tel: 09 523 1318. Fax: 09 534 7201. E-mail: *imigr8@leggetibis.com* Website: *www.leggitibis.com* Specialises in employment search and relocation at business, professional and executive level, family reunification and all NZ immigration and citizenship requirements.

Lothian Consultants Limited, 45a Bleakhouse Road, Howick, Auckland. Tel: 09 535 6811.

Lucas France & Partners, National Bank House, 6 Osterley Way, Manakua, Auckland. Tel: 09 262 2142. Fax: 09 262 2194. Professional immigration lawyers providing complete legal services connected with permanent residence, business, general and family migration.

Malcolm Pacific International Ltd, Level 7, 70 Symonds Street, PO Box 6219, Wellesley Street, Auckland. Tel: 09 309 4187. Fax: 09 366 4730. Website: *www.malcolmpacific.co.nz* Free consultation and assessment and money-back guarantee.

Marshall Bird Immigration Ltd, Level 7, 17 Albert Street, Auckland. Tel: 09 373 3165. Lawyers specialising in obtaining work permits and permanent residence in New Zealand.

New Horizons, PO Box 11-125, Ellerslie. Tel: 09 525 4052. Services include: immigration solutions, professional registration assistance and translations. Mandarin and European languages spoken.

New Zealand Association for Migration and Investment, 71

Devonport Road, PO Box 518, Tauranga. Tel: 07 578 1883.
New Zealand Immigration and Investment Services, 5/138 Queen
Street, Auckland. Tel: 09 366 0378.
North Shore Immigration Service Ltd, 7 Pierce Road, Milford,
Auckland. Tel: 09 486 7100. Fax: 09 486 7101. Website:
*www.nsis.co.nz* Free assessment interview for applications of
residence.
Prospects Immigration, PO Box 38-880, Howick. Tel: 09 534 1961.
Fax: 09 534 1965. Specialists in permanent residence and work
permit applications and job search. Free assessment.
Tika Ram Immigration Consultants, 3$^{rd}$ Floor, S302A, Dilworth
Building, 24 corner of Queen and Customs Streets. Tel: 09 379
0387. Fax: 09 358 1728.
Turner Hopkins, 400 Lake Road, Takapuna. Tel: 09 486 2169. Fax:
09 486 2160. For assistance with immigration problems including
applications and appeals.
WASAN International Co Ltd, BNZ Tower, Floor 9, 125 Queen
Street, Auckland. Tel: 09 308 9998. Email: *immigration@*
*bizonglobe.com* Immigration specialists dealing with permanent
residency, appeals, work permits, student and visitor's permits
and job search.
Worldwide Immigration Services Ltd, Level 12, 242 Queen Street,
Auckland. Tel: 09 358 0884.

**Christchurch**
Brockett; James, 77 Hereford Street, Christchurch. Tel: 03 366 1487.
A firm of barristers and solicitors offering professional advice.
Business Immigration (NZ) Limited, PO Box 2286, Christchurch.
Tel: 03 341 3340. Members of the New Zealand Association for
migration and investment and specialists in permanent residency.
Lane Neave Ronaldson, Price Waterhouse Centre, 119 Armagh
Street, Christchurch. Tel: 03 379 3720. Fax: 03 379 8370.
Specialising in all matters relating to residency applications
(points system, business investment, family category and
humanitarian).
New Zealand Immigration Ltd, PO Box 11-073, Christchurch. Tel:
03 365 3306. Fax: 03 365 3460. Email: *forbes@net2.co.nz*
Investment and permanent residence applications.
Weston Ward and Lascelles, 211 Gloucester Street, Christchurch.
Tel: 03 379 1740 or call free: 0800 529 937. Fax: 03 379 1789. A
firm of barristers and solicitors providing advice on application
problems.

## Wellington

Execucorp Migration Services, 49 Ridgeway, Wanganui. Tel: 06 347 2776. Advises on all immigration matters including visas, work permits and New Zealand residency.

Malcolm Pacific, 276 Lambton Quay, Wellington. Tel: 04 473 9615. Fax: 04 499 6559. Offers professional service for migrants and employers, free assessments. Performance guarantee independently underwritten by professional indemnity insurance company.

Thomas and Associates, PO Box 31-160, Lower Hutt, Wellington. Tel: 04 939 8466.

## PROFESSIONAL ASSOCIATIONS

### Wellington

New Zealand Association of Occupational Therapists, PO Box 12-506, Thorndon. Tel: 04 473 6510.

New Zealand Computer Society, Paxus House, 73 Boulcott Street, Wellington. Tel: 04 473 1043. Fax: 04 473 1025.

New Zealand Medical Association, PO Box 156, Wellington. Tel: 04 472 4741. Fax: 04 471 0838. Email: *nzma@nzma.org.nz* Website: *www.nzma.org.nz*

New Zealand Minerals Industry Association, PO Box 5039, Wellington. Tel: 04 499 9871. Fax: 04 499 9873. Email: *nzmia@xtra.co.nz* Website: *www.minerals.co.nz*

New Zealand Police Association Inc, 57 Willis Street, Wellington. Tel: 04 472 0198. Fax: 04 471 1309.

New Zealand Recreation Association, 14 Frankmore Avenue, Johnsonville, Wellington. Tel: 04 478 3814. Fax: 04 478 5237.

New Zealand University Students Association, 354 Lambton Quay, PO Box 10-191, Wellington. Tel: 04 498 2500. Fax: 04 473 2391.

Petroleum Exploration Association of New Zealand, PO Box 5227, Wellington. Tel: 04 472 1933. Fax: 04 472 3968.

Pharmaceutical Society of New Zealand, 124 Dixon Street, Wellington. Tel: 04 802 0030. Fax: 04 382 9397.

### Auckland

Chartered Institute of Transport, 298a Wairau Road, Glenfield. Tel: 09 444 4261.

## TRADE AND/OR INDUSTRY ASSOCIATIONS

### Wellington

AGCARM Agricultural Chemical and Animal Remedies Manufacturers Association of New Zealand Inc, 12 Johnston Street, Wellington. Tel: 04 499 4225. Fax: 04 499 4223.

Aviation Industry Association of New Zealand Inc, Agriculture House, 12 Johnston Street, Wellington. Tel: 04 472 2707.

Booksellers New Zealand, 86 Boulcott Street, Wellington. Tel: 04 472 8678.

Bus and Coach Association (NZ) Ltd, 05 Williams and Adams Building, 79 Boulcott Street, PO Box 9336, Wellington. Tel: 04 499 7334.

Deer Farmers Association, Level 10, 101 Lambton Quay, Wellington. Tel: 04 472 5092. Fax: 04 472 5151.

Hospitality Association of New Zealand, Education House, 178-182 Willis Street, Wellington. Tel: 04 385 1369.

Independent Schools Council, PO Box 5222, Wellington. Tel: 04 471 2022.

Insurance Institute of New Zealand Inc, Guardian Assurance House, 111-115 Custom House Quay, Wellington. Tel: 04 499 4630. Fax: 04 499 4536.

Itanz (Information and Technology Association of NZ Inc), 9th Floor, 108 The Terrace, PO Box 1710, Wellington. Tel: 04 472 2731. Fax: 04 499 3318. Email: *info@itanz.org.nz* Website: *www.itanz.org.nz*

Motor Trade Association Inc, 32-34 Kent Terrace, PO Box 9244, Wellington. Tel: 04 385 8859. Fax: 04 385 9517. Email: *mta@motor-trade.co.nz* Website: *www.mta.org.nz*

NZ Bankers Association, Level 12, Grand Arcade Tower, 16 Willis Street, PO Box 3043, Wellington. Tel: 04 472 8838. Fax: 04 473 1698. Email: *acopland@nzba.org.nz*

NZ Berryfruit Growers Federation Inc, 12 Johnston Street, Wellington. Tel: 04 473 5387.

NZ Chambers of Commerce, Level 9, 109 Featherston Street, PO Box 11-043, Wellington. Tel: 04 472 2725.

NZ Chemical Industry Council Inc, Agriculture House, 12 Johnston Street, Wellington. Tel: 04 499 4311. Fax: 04 472 7100.

NZ Employers Federation, 15-17 Murphy Street, Thorndon, PO Box 1786. Tel: 04 499 4111. Fax: 04 499 4112. Email: *nzef@nzef.org.nz*

NZ Painting Contractors Association (Inc), 63 Miramar Avenue,

Miramar. Tel: 04 388 1516.

New Zealand Retail Meat and Allied Trades Federation, Molesworth House, 101-103 Molesworth Street, Wellington. Tel: 04 472 0807. Fax: 04 472 0804. Email: *enquiry@retailmeat.org.nz*

New Zealand Meat Industry Association (Inc), Wool House, 10 Brando Street, PO Box 345, Wellington. Tel: 04 473 6465.

New Zealand Timber Industry Federation Inc, 2 Maginnity Street, Wellington. Tel: 04 473 5200.

New Zealand Tourism Industry Association, 4th Floor, Paxus House, 79 Boulcott Street, Welllington. Tel: 04 499 0104. Fax: 04 499 0827. Email: *nztia@xtra.co.nz*

Nursery and Garden Industry Association of New Zealand (Inc), PO Box 3443, Wellington. Tel: 04 385 3511.

Pharmacy Guild of New Zealand Inc, National Headquarters, Pharmacy House, 124 Dixon Street, Wellington. Tel: 04 385 8200.

Printing Industries NZ, Huddart Parker Building, Post Office Square, Wellington. Tel: 04 472 3497 Fax: 04 472 3534

Researched Medicines Industry Association NZ Inc, Level 8, Castrol House, 36 Custom House Quay, PO Box 10-447, Wellington. Tel: 04 499 4277.

Vegetable and Potato Growers Federation (Inc), Huddart Parker Building, Post Office Square, Wellington. Tel: 04 472 3795. Fax: 04 471 2861. Email: *information@vedfed.co.nz*

Wellington Regional Chamber of Commerce, Level 9, 109 Featherston Street, PO Box 1590, Wellington. Tel: 04 472 2725. Fax: 04 471 1767. Email: *info@wgtn-chamber.co.nz* Website: *www.wgtn-chamber.co.nz*

### Christchurch

Canterbury Employers Chamber of Commerce, 57 Kilmore Street, Christchurch. Tel: 03 366 5096.

Canterbury Manufacturers Association Inc, corner of Cambridge Terrace and Manchester Street, Christchurch. Tel: 03 366 5993.

Canterbury Hotel Association, Floor 1, 96 Tuam Street, Christchurch. Tel: 03 379 5193.

New Zealand Institute of Management Canterbury Division, 307 Madras Street, PO Box 13-044, Christchurch. Tel: 03 379 2302. Fax: 03 366 7069. Email: *canty@nzim.co.nz* Website: *www.nzim.co.nz*

NZ Road Transport Association, 41 Carlyle Street, Christchurch. Tel: 03 366 9854.

Retail Merchants Association, PO Box 13-877, Christchurch. Tel: 03

366 1308

## Auckland

Recording Industry Association of New Zealand, 11 York Street, PO Box 37-442, Auckland. Tel: 09 308 0510. Fax: 09 306 4977.

# Glossary

## EMPLOYMENT RELATED TERMS

| | |
|---|---|
| CV | Curriculum Vitae |
| Env | Environment |
| Exp'd | Experienced |
| Exc | Excellent |
| o'time | Overtime |
| Opp | Opportunity |
| Gvt | Government |
| CA | Chartered Accountant |
| Reqd | Required |
| Tech | Technical |
| Immed | Immediate |
| d/licence | Drivers Licence |
| Snr | Senior |
| Asst | Assistant |
| Pref | Prefer |
| PA | Personal Assistant |

## NEW ZILDISH

| | |
|---|---|
| counselled out | a new terminology for making someone redundant |
| chook | chicken |
| red beet | beetroot |
| she'll be right | everything will be fine |
| togs & cossies | swim suits |
| smoko | tea break |
| barbie | barbecue |
| mozzie | mosquito |
| blow fly | bluebottle |
| Aussieland | Australia |
| sickie | sick day off work |

| | |
|---|---|
| chippie | carpenter |
| having a zzz | having a sleep |
| possie | position |
| gummies | gum boots (wellingtons) |
| footie | football |
| kindy | kindergarten |
| pakeha | Maori name for a European |
| ciggies | cigarettes |
| wobblies | tantrums |
| snarlers | sausages |
| this arvo | this afternoon |
| surfie | surf board rider |
| lollies | sweets and candies |
| posties | the postman |
| rough as guts | crude, unrefined, impolite |
| cobber | friend |
| strike me pink | surprise or disbelief |
| up your nose with a rubber hose | scorn |
| gidday | hello |
| major | something big and important |
| oh O.K. } yeh O.K. } | I understand, I see |
| bach | seaside cottage |
| a blue | a mistake |
| rark up | be loud and raucous |
| scarfie | a university student |
| shanky | unreliable, unsafe |
| shoot through | to leave quickly |
| tiki-tour | cheap sightseeing tour |
| hard yacker | hard work |
| towie | tow-truck driver |
| untold | a large number of |
| spit the dummy | have a fit of anger |

# Useful Addresses

## NEW ZEALAND EMPLOYMENT SERVICE

National Office: PO Box 3705, Wellington.

## TREATY OF WAITANGI INFORMATION

The Information Section, Waitangi Tribunal Division, Department of Justice, PO Box 10-044, Wellington, New Zealand.

## NEW ZEALAND IMMIGRATION

### NZ offices

New Zealand Immigration Service, Private Bag, Wellesley Street, Auckland.
New Zealand Immigration Service, Private Bag, Hamilton.
New Zealand Immigration Service, PO Box 948, Palmerston North.
New Zealand Immigration Service, PO Box 27149, Upper Willis Street, Wellington.
New Zealand Immigration Service, PO Box 22111, Christchurch.
New Zealand Immigration Service, PO Box 557, Dunedin.

### Overseas offices

New Zealand Consulate-General, Springiedelgasse 28, A-1190 Wien, Austria.
NZ Consulate Generale, 1 Alfred Street, Circular Quay, GPO Box 365, Sydney, NSW 2000, Australia.
New Zealand High Commission, Suite 801, Metropolitan House, 99 Bank Street, Ottawa, Ontario Klp 6G3, Canada.
New Zealand Consulate-General, Suite 1200-888 Dunsmuir Street, (PO Box 10071, Pacific Centre) Vancouver, BC V6C 3K4, Canada.
New Zealand Embassy, 7 ter, Leonard de Vinci, 75116, Paris,

France.

NZ Embassy, Bonn Centre H 1902, Bundeskanzlerplatz 2–10, 53113 Bonn, Germany.

NZ Embassy, Carnegielaan 10, 2517 HD The Hague, The Netherlands.

NZ High Commission, 391A Orchard Road, 15–05 Tower A, Ngee Ann City, Singapore 0923.

New Zealand Consulate-General, 28A Chemin du Petit-Saconnex, CH-1209 Geneva (PO Box 334, CH-1211, Geneva 19), Switzerland.

NZ High Commission, New Zealand House, 80 Haymarket, London SW1Y 4TE.

New Zealand Embassy, 37 Observatory Circle NW, Washington, DC 20008, United States of America.

New Zealand Consulate-General, Suite 1530, Tishman Buildings, 15th Floor, 10960 Wilshire Boulevard, Los Angeles, CA 90024, United States of America.

## GENERAL INFORMATION ABOUT NEW ZEALAND

Auckland Information Centre, Aotea Square, Queen Street, Auckland.

Wellington Public Relations Office, Cnr Victoria & Wakefield Street, Wellington.

Hamilton Visitor Centre, Angelsea Street, Hamilton.

New Plymouth Public Relations & Marketing Office, Private Bag 2025, New Plymouth.

Christchurch Information Centre, Worcester Street/Oxford Terrace, Christchurch.

## HELPFUL ADDRESSES

New Zealand Computer Society, NZIG House, 133 The Terrace, Wellington.

New Zealand Association of Language Teachers, PO Box 12 237 Thorndon, Wellington.

New Zealand Association of Occupational Therapists, PO Box 12–506, Thorndon, Wellington.

New Zealand Association of Optometrists, PO Box 30545, Lower Hutt, Wellington.

New Zealand College of Clinical Psychologists, PO Box 16–033,

Wellington South.

New Zealand College of Physiotherapy Inc., 197 Willis Street, Wellington.

New Zealand Customs Department, PO Box 2218, Wellington

*New Zealand Engineering News*, Lindis Manor, 4 Lindis Close, Kelson, Wellington.

# Further Reading

## BOOKS

*The New Zealand Experience: A World Model for Structural Adjustment*, Jane Kelsey, (Collins).

*A Critical View of the Relationship*, Raj Vasil.

*The Strategic & Economic Outlook*, Terence O'Brien and Sir Frank Holmes (Collins).

*Redemption Songs*, Judith Binney (Auckland University Press).

*Making the Difference*, Ruth Richardson (Shoal Bay Press).

*Politics in New Zealand*, Richard Mulgan (Auckland University Press).

*New Zealand & China Towards 2000*, Lindsay Watt (Victoria University Press).

*The Economics of Markets: A New Zealand Perspective*, Michael Pickford (Dunmore Press).

*The New Zealand Economy*, Stuart Birks & Srikanmta Chatterjee (Dunmore Press).

*The Vision and the Reality: Equal Employment Opportunities in the New Zealand Workplace*, Janet Sayers and Marianne Tremain (Dunmore Press).

*Gender Culture and Power*, Bev James & Kay Saville-Smith (Oxford University Press).

*New Zealand Society*, Paul Spoonley, David Pearson & Ian Shirley (Dunmore Press).

*Unbridled Power*, Geoffrey Palmer (Oxford University Press).

*All Honourable Men*, Hugh Templeton (Auckland University Press).

*Counting for Nothing*, Marilyn Waring (Allen Unwin NZ Ltd).

*Unfinished Business*, Roger Douglas (Random House).

*Constitution in Crisis*, Geoffrey Palmer (John McIndoe).

*History of New Zealand*, Keith Sinclair (Penguin Books).

*Education is Change*, Harvey McQuenn (Bridget Williams Books Ltd).

*Immigration and National Identity in New Zealand*, Stuart W Greif

(Dunmore Press).

*The Logic of New Zealand Business*, Robert T Hamilton & Gurvinder Singh Shergill (Oxford University Press).

*Violence in New Zealand*, Jane & James Ritchie (Huia Publishers, Daphne Brasell Associates Press).

*Aotearoa and New Zealand*, Alan Grey (Canterbury University Press).

*Travesty of Waitangi*, Stuart C Scott (The Campbell Press, Dunedin).

*A Guide to the Ski Areas in New Zealand*, Marty Sharpe (Random House).

*Golfing in New Zealand*, Jim Wallace (Cosmos Tourist Guide Books).

*The New Zealand Bed & Breakfast Book*, J & J Thomas (Moonshine Press).

*New Zealand Camping Guide*, Gay Kerr & Noni Hansen (T. O. W. Travels).

*New Zealand: A Language Survival Kit*, Carolyn Catt (Longman Paul).

## PERIODICALS

*Destination New Zealand*, Outbound Newspapers, 1 Commercial Road, Eastbourne, East Sussex BN21 3XQ. Tel: (01323) 412001. Fax: (01323) 649249.

*New Zealand News UK*, PO Box 10, Berwick on Tweed, Northumberland TD15 1BW.

*New Zealand Outlook*, Consyl Publishing, 3 Buckhurst Road, Bexhill-on-Sea, Sussex TN40 1QF. Tel: (01424) 223111. Fax: (01424) 224992.

# Index

Accident compensation, 113
Accidents, 59
Accommodation, 69
Accountancy, 81
Accounts, 94, 97
Addresses, 138
Advantages, 118
Advertising, 80
Age points, 45
Agriculture, 82
Automotive engineers, 84
Aviation, 81

Beauty, 85
Building trades, 84

Catering, 85
Checklist, 119
Chiropractors, 86
Cinemas, 71
CIT, 109
Cities, 17
Clerical, 94
Climate, 16
Computing, 86
CV, 76

Dental treatment, 113
Dentistry, 86
Direct investment, 43

Disadvantages, 118
Doctors, 91
Dress, 72

Economists, 88
Economy, 20
Employment terms, 135
English language, 41

Family sponsorship, 39
Family support benefit, 67
Fruit growing areas, 18
Funds, transfer, 47

Hairdressing, 85
Health, 89
Health care, 112
Hospitals, 113

Immigration trends, 25
Income, overseas, 64
Industry, 93

Job leads, 79

Law, 93
Lecturers, 87
Legal, 95

Maori phrases, 14

Marketing, 95
Maternity leave, 56
Medical insurance, 115
Migrant levy, 40
Ministry of Health, 112

New Zildish, 135
Nursing, 92

Operation costs, 116
Optometrists, 98

Pensions, 67
Permanent migrants, 33
Permits, 26
Personal grievance, 55
Personnel consultants, 101
Pharmacists, 98
Physiotherapists, 99
Podiatrists, 100
Polytechnics, 109
Population, 17
Population trends, 15
Professionals, 98
Professors, 87
Psychologists, 100
Pubs, 71

Qualification points, 42
Qualification requirements, 105

Real estate agents, 100
Receptionists, 94, 97
Redundancy, 22
Refusal, 27
Regional health authorities, 112
Restaurants, 71

Sales, staff, 95, 96, 97
Schools, 69
Secretarial, 94, 97
Settlement factors and funds, 38
Signing a contract, 53
Smokefree, 58
Sport, 72
Students, 28
Surveyors, 100

Taxation, 62
Tax, company, 65
Tax, double, 66
Tax, exemptions, 63
Tax, fringe benefits, 66
Tax, Goods & Services, 64
Teachers, 87
Technical, 97
Technician courses, 110
Technology, 97
Trade courses, 110
Training, 107
Treaty of Waitangi, 13

Unemployment, 21
Unions, 54
University, 107

Valuers, 101
Veterinarians, 101
Visas, 26
Visitors, 27
Visitors visa, 31

Workers, 30
Work experience points, 39
Working holidays, 32
Work permits, 26

Printed in Great Britain
by Amazon

44489143R00084